THE REVERSE QUARANTINE

Nadakkavu, Kozhikode, Kerala, 673011
www.insightpublica.com
e-mail: insightpublica@gmail.com
Title: THE REVERSE QUARANTINE
Author: Charunainika
Illustrations: Charunainika
First Edition: February 2025

Printed and Published by
InsightinPublica Printers & Publishers Pvt. Ltd.
ISBN - 978-93-5517-732-2
₹200/-

THE REVERSE QUARANTINE

CHARUNAINIKA

INSIGHT PUBLICA®

To my beloved maternal grandparents,

Here's to you not just as family but as cherished friends with whom I've shared countless memories, stories, and unforgettable days. From the tales you've told to the games we've played, every moment spent with you, from my earliest years to my teenage days, has strengthened our bond and filled my life with joy.

Thank you for your constant love, support, and for always being by my side. I am forever grateful for everything you've done and for the incredible moments we've shared.

With Love
Charu

Editor's Note

It's a rare and wondrous thing to encounter a voice as fresh, insightful, and authentic as Charunainika 's. At just 13 years old, she has penned "The Reverse Quarantine," a poignant and often humorous coming-of-age story that captures the unique and unsettling experience of adolescence during the COVID-19 pandemic.

This isn't just another pandemic narrative. While the backdrop of lockdowns, masks, and social distancing undeniably shapes the story, "The Reverse Quarantine" delves deeper. It's a captivating exploration of identity, friendship, and the anxieties that come with navigating the murky waters of teenage life.

Charu's protagonist, Shivani, a relatable and endearing character, grapples with the familiar challenges of school, friendships, and family dynamics, all while contending with the unprecedented disruptions of the pandemic. We witness her struggles with online learning, the loneliness of isolation, and the anxieties surrounding the invisible enemy lurking outside.

But "The Reverse Quarantine" is far from a bleak portrayal of hardship. It's a celebration of resilience, creativity, and the enduring power of human connection. Charu masterfully captures the moments of joy and laughter that emerged amidst the chaos – the newfound appreciation for family time, the blossoming of unexpected friendships, exploration of online platforms, and the discovery of hidden talents and passions.

The writing in "The Reverse Quarantine" is a revelation. Charu possesses a remarkable maturity and a keen eye for detail. Her prose is both lyrical and insightful, effortlessly conveying the emotional nuances of teenage life. Her humor is sharp and witty, injecting much-needed levity into a sometimes heavy subject matter.

What truly sets "The Reverse Quarantine" apart is its authenticity. This is a story told from the heart, a genuine reflection of a generation grappling with a crisis unlike any other. Charu's voice is honest, unfiltered, and undeniably her own. She speaks directly to her peers, offering a much-needed sense of shared experience and validation.

"The Reverse Quarantine" is a powerful testament to the resilience of the human spirit. It's a reminder that even in the darkest of times, hope and joy can always be found. This book will undoubtedly resonate with young readers, offering a valuable perspective on a pivotal moment in history.

Charunainika is a rising star. With "The Reverse Quarantine," her second foray into fiction writing, she has not only crafted a compelling and insightful coming-of-age story, but has also given voice to an entire generation. This is a book that will stay with readers long after they turn the final page.

Beyond the literary merit, "The Reverse Quarantine" holds significant entertainment value. It serves as a unique and invaluable document of this unprecedented time in history. This book offers a window into the lived experiences of very young people during the COVID-19 pandemic, capturing their anxieties, their frustrations, and their hopes for the future.

In a world that often overlooks the voices of young people, "The Reverse Quarantine" rovides a much-needed platform for their perspectives to be heard. Charu's story is a powerful reminder of the importance of listening to young people, understanding their unique challenges, and supporting their emotional well-being.

" The Reverse Quarantine" is a reminder that even in the face of adversity, creativity and resilience can flourish. Charunainika has given us a gift – a poignant, insightful, and ultimately hopeful story that will continue to resonate for years to come.

This book is a must-read for anyone who wants to understand the impact of the pandemic on a generation, and a source of inspiration for young writers everywhere.

I am proud to have had the privilege of working with Charu on this remarkable novel.

Sincerely,

Dr. Arunlal Mokeri

A pandemic births hope

Grandparents always have an interesting way around kids but unfortunately, thanks to modern, busy, urban, nuclear lifestyles, what we see is not just kids moving rapidly away from their grandparents, rather grandparents forcibly adjusting to confine themselves within 'boxes'. The Reverse Quarantine is a story of the 'positive' effects of Covid-19 and how little Charunainika makes use of her 'scary' time to make it totally positive. When the pandemic had the entire world in its grip, people were scared that they would never be able to return to their normal lives for the next five years. The story explores how the writer was able to bond with cats, fish and nature in general along with her maternal grandparents. The very title 'The Reverse Quarantine' expresses it all – what was expected to be a quite boring, unprepared and fearful time was converted into an interesting, and adventurous period, where despite being quarantined, people bonded more with nature, otherwise missing in their lives.

The 'surprises' that her 'grampa' throws also amazes the readers, making the book more appealing to all age groups. It is quite interesting to be reminded once again that children are great observers and as such, they are still able to empathise with elders, viewing things from their perspective. It is revealing that instead of being glued to screens in tiny hands, the current generation has not abandoned the joys of reading and writing. Charunainika through the protagonist, Shivani, never shies away from baring her insecurities to the readers, lending more depth to the work.

Whether it is Covid-19, or any other contagion, life has its own positive and negative turning points and it is left to us to choose whether we lead lives of despair, or brimming with hope. A tender Charu, pushing teenage, impacts the readers through this wonderful work, blending both sensitivity and maturity in handling things outside of her control. We often blame a lot of things averring that nothing here is ever going to change, though the power lies in oneself – a deep philosophical insight ensconced in her little world reflected in the maxim: "The World changes when YOU change".

I am sure that readers will gain as much happiness as I have in reading these pages.

It is my pleasure to wish all the very best to

Charunainika, an esteemed student of Silver Hills Higher Secondary School, and hope she blossoms into a great writer!

Fr John Mannarathara CMI

Principal, Silver Hills HSS

Paroppadi, Kozhikkode

FOREWORD

When I visited Silver Hills HSS last year, I was given a copy of The Unknown Friend, a book written by Charunainika, a ten-year-old class V student. One quick glance, and I realised the book isn't a run-of-the mill story but a unique piece of work. So when I was asked to write the foreword for Charunainika's second novel, I readily agreed for I was certain the book would be unusual. And I wasn't wrong.

If I was surprised that a ten-year-old could write a book like The Unknown Friend, I was amazed that a thirteen year-old could come out with a novel that deftly combines realism with magic. The Reverse Quarantine is not just a story set during Covid times, with its fears and challenges, but it is a stream of consciousness narration that delves into the mind of a ten year old, her relationship with her family, friends and pets, her musings about the universe, science and religion, her dreams, her fantasies, her struggles, her failures and triumphs.

The Reverse Quarantine, written in the first person by the protagonist, Shivani, a fifth grader of Oak Leaf School, reads like a journal. It is quite likely, though, that there are a lot of autobiographical elements in the book. It starts with the disturbing announcement on television of a new virus, COVID-19, that turned the whole world upside down, and ends with the welcome lifting of the restrictions. But it is not a mundane record of events that happened in Shivani's life during that period, but a lively back and forth account of anything that catches the fancy of Shivani with her thoughts zigzagging their way through the past, the present and the future.

The Covid restrictions come as a big bow to Shivani. As she says, 'All my plans are DESTROYED.' No hangouts with friends, no going to school, no delightful vacation... Instead the family goes to stay with Shivani's grandparents at their village, which has transformed from a bustling place into an eerily silent one. Shivani brings out the fears that assail all of them, but every incident, every thought, takes her to related topics, reminiscences and fanciful daydreams. Her love-hate relationship with her cousins, her love for animals and all creatures, her concern for her grandparents, her passion for cats and for art, her views on scientists, the universe, the environment, her experiences in school and random funny incidents, are narrated in a unique style with refreshing charm, humour and an admirable command of the language, which is occasionally peppered with the lingo of Gen Z.

I especially liked Shivani's concern for her grandfather's memory that makes her regularly give him one sentence of a story with some key words to memorise, and how her 75-year-old grandfather strings together the whole story in a letter given to her just before the family leaves for their city after the restrictions are lifted. Does it reveal his fantastic memory, or is it a confession? Whatever it is, it brings the book to a neat close with the meaningful assertion, 'the world changes when you change.' The book makes it clear it is not the other way about.

Charunainika is not just an artist with words. Her artistry extends to sketching and her charming illustrations add to the appeal of the book. The Reverse Quarantine was an eye-opener for me in more ways than one and I totally enjoyed reading it.

With her obvious talents, her vision and her distinctive approach to writing at such a tender age, Charunainika is bound to go places. I wish her all the best and a very creative future.

KHYRUNNISA A.

Charunainika, a budding young author from Calicut, Kerala, is the daughter of Anjali Chandran and Laju G L. Her passion for stories and books has been the driving force behind her creative journey, fostering a deep love for literature and storytelling.

An avid reader, Charu has explored children's literature in both English and Malayalam, which inspired her to begin writing. Her debut novella, The Unknown Friend, published in 2022, showcases her vivid imagination and features her own illustrations, adding a unique touch to her work.

In 2023, she received the prestigious Ujjwala Balyam award, instituted by the Women and Child Development Department, Government of Kerala. She also demonstrated her talent at the Kerala State School Kalolsavam, earning an A grade in English Upanasyam. Currently a student in the 8th grade at Silver Hills HSS, Charu continues to inspire others with her creativity and passion for storytelling.

She can be reached at doodlecharu@gmail.com.

Charunainika

CONTENTS

THINGS DON'T ALWAYS GO AS PLANNED 21
WELCOME TO IAP 29
FADING COLOURS 35
VISHU 42
THE TELEPHONE BOOK & MY COUSINS 48
QUARANTINE 54
BIRD WATER SUPPLY 59
AN UNFORGETTABLE LOSS 65
THE MUSHROOM DEN 70
PARACETAMOL 75
MY BIRTHDAY 79
HOW MY GRAMMA CAUGHT A TURTLE 84
BUTTERFLY HATCHERY 88
ONLINE ONAM 93
POPPY THE DEAD 101
BAD HAIR-DAY 107
CAMPFIRE, HOT CHOCOLATE, AND A CHRISTMAS EVE 110
VACCINATIONS AND MY DEATHLY FEAR OF NEEDLES 116
COPYCATS 121
A MIME'S STORY 125
EVERYTHING MUST COME TO AN END 128

01

THINGS DON'T ALWAYS GO AS PLANNED

Dear viewers,

A new virus named COVID-19 has been found in Wuhan, China. Students and immigrants from other countries living in China are being sent back to their home countries. The Chinese government has put other countries at risk because the chance of immigrants carrying the virus is high. The infection carries symptoms like headache, sneezing, cough and stomach-ache. To avoid contracting Covid, wear a mask, use sanitizer, and follow a social distance of six feet. Further updates will be reported."

These words – uttered by a random news reader – were the words I woke up to that day. I was still not completely out of the world of my dreams.

"The price of masks and sanitizer and even stuff needed in our daily lives are skyrocketing. Yesterday, the entire section for the chocolate spread ran out. I had to buy a nut thing instead. I hope Shivani likes it, she usually doesn't. Hey, today I have to go early to work. Also yes, you can hang out today with your friends from half-past two to three. I have ironed your uniform and have kept it in the closet. Bye! Love you!"

"Ugh – Can I sleep for just 5 more minutes, Mum?" I blurted out.

"You are currently studying in 5th grade, young lady, please be more responsible and don't make me repeat this. Do you want me to shout or could you just wake up now?"

"Okay, " I grunted.

Fast-forward a bit:

Let me introduce myself to you.

In...

3.2.1...Let's go!

Hi, my name is Shivani and I am studying in 5th grade. I am studying at this school named Oak Leaf School. If you think bullies, noisy children, clique groups, intense competition for popularity, production centre of teacher's pets, wannabe princesses, social media so-called celebrities, ego-clash warriors, nerds-n-whizzes & drama queens, and food fights are posh and amazing, then welcome to your paradise.

After hearing what Mum said you might think I am a reckless child but I am an okay kid. I swear I am. She wants me to wake up at five in the morning, and on most days I'm good with that. Every morning, I walk to school with the other kids. We have a lot to study, compared to other schools. All my cousins are fortunate to be in a regular school rather than this one that smothers you in homework. Not to brag but I can solve a Rubik's cube in less than two minutes and I score impressive marks in exams.

My mother is a graphic designer and my dad is a software engineer and a home cook, he likes cooking but he says it's annoying to think of it all the time. They are sure that I have both of their skills. My life is stuck in a very crammed villa in the same neighbourhood where my school is.

You see, when you think of the word "villa" you may think of either

Option 1. Vanilla but spelled without "an".

Option 1.5 Villain but spelled without "in".

Option 2. A shrunk futuristic home with a nice view outside and blah, blah, blah, blah, blah with many other similar clones surrounding it.

Or alas, Option 3. A villa is just a small house with a posh name.

Sadly, number 3 wasn't lucky this time so yes, Option 3 is the right answer (sigh)

So, you might think I hate my school and I just want to move out of that villa. Well, no, I–I yeah. I do kind of hate this school. Significantly on a day like today. You see, this was an exam week, and since our school made the exams, some kind of issue took place, and they thought– "HA! Let them re-write the hardest exams and yada, yada, yada." So that means an extra week of exams. WHICH MEANS a whole week taken from our summer vacations. My friend Gowri withdrew her trip to Panaji, where the rest of her family is now. Yep, it is literally a disaster.

We got to go home in the boiling afternoon. And our teacher said to come in the early morning because they want to have an assembly based on some sort of topic, I dunno. I am passionate about cooking and I experiment with different kinds of foods.

Since we live near an all-you-need supermarket, a few meters from home, I use my pocket money every weekend to purchase stuff with my parents. And my uncle works there – if I impress him, (which isn't as hard as you think) he will let me buy a few more things. So, I would not forget to keep my Rubik's cube in my bag. And sometimes we will get a coupon for being a frequent customer. I will use it to purchase some cooking supplies and other stuff to live on, because you can't live only with cooking supplies. If I was able to, I certainly would.

Last week, we purchased a packet of chocolate chips and used them to create a batch of delicious, untouched cookies. I made an ample quantity, enough to share one each with my two friends. Despite this, I assure you that I am NOT lacking in the friend-making department. I have a considerable number of friends with whom I willingly share my cherished treats; however, I typically choose the top two to receive such special offerings. In addition to my culinary endeavors, I have a passion for drawing. While some may opt for peculiar studies involving 3D shapes and light distribution, I prefer sketching the tree outside, intertwined with the swings. Occasionally, I spend time with my friends after securing permission the day before. This usually involves activities like feeding fish and birds, driven by my desire to care for pets that I don't currently own.

I've observed our inquisitive neighbour, Sushama, walking her dog at seven in the morning, precisely when I embark on my journey to school, reaching there within a five-minute span. School commences at half-past seven, and we are granted a one-hour lunch break. I collaborate with my parents to prepare my lunch, often opting for pasta due to my fondness for it.

Today being our hangout day, my friends and I initially planned to visit the park with Gowri's college-going sister. However, our plans took an unexpected turn, prompting us to shift to plan B – a visit to the supermarket I frequent. Fortunately, I had a coupon and happily purchased some chips before deciding to head home.

Meanwhile, Sushama stuck to her routine of walking her dog in circles around the neighbourhood, seemingly on a quest for fresh gossip to share with her friends. It's moments like these that intensify my dislike for her.

As for vacations, Gosh! I had grand plans this time around! In the usual 10-week break, I had envisioned dedicating a week to theme parks, nearly a month for extensive travel and indulging in various cuisines, two weeks for visiting grandmas, and the remaining time for school reopening preparations. However, due to this nuisance... I believe some adjustments might be necessary.I went inside and finished my homework. I switched on our television and I got shivers down my spine."Dear viewers

We are back again with the covid virus. For those who don't know, it has symptoms like headache, sneezing, cough, stomach-ache, etc. To avoid this, wear a mask, use sanitizer, and follow a social distance of 2m (6ft). We appreciate kids under 12 and elders over 60 not going out. Please stock food for a week. Working will be online through work from home. Strict lockdown is followed and shops will only be open from 9 am to 7 pm. The lockdown will start tomorrow. Only grocery shops and pharmacies will be opened. All other shops are closed till further notice. Movie theatres and theme parks will be closed. People will be restricted from going out of the state or country by the most. If you have to, a form must be filled out. The form will be supplied with the everyday delivery of newspaper.

We are going on a short break. Thank you."

"Why does it look like the entire world is in trouble, why? All my plans are DESTROYED" I said, confused.

I saw Mum and Dad with the same sad, confused, and angry faces. Both of them came near and tightly hugged me. I think we are in very big trouble.

This turn of events compelled us to vacate the villa, where we had a neighbouring woman with slightly erratic tendencies and her dog. My parents, driven by concerns about the Nipah virus outbreak, were visibly distressed, fearing a scenario akin to the severity of the Nipah times. Their primary worry was leaving my grandparents vulnerable. Consequently, we made the decision to seek refuge at my grandma's house. However, the drawback of this relocation would be the dusty walls and cupboards at the grandma's. It doesn't worry me, but it is a significant issue for my mother who suffers from a severe dust allergy. *ACHOO! ACHOO!*

In preparation for our move, we packed all essential

Itfeltas if we
were...alone

items. My mother insisted on bringing her art supplies, my father opted to carry his cooking equipment, and I, without hesitation, gathered my entire hoard. Almost forgetting my pillow, I quickly grabbed it before leaving. Following my mother's strong desire to capture the scenic beauty, we also decided to bring our filming set. The majority opinion ruled, and we packed accordingly.

The situation in the outside world was grim, with supermarkets, hospitals, and various other places being entirely depleted, especially in terms of masks and sanitizers. Even my parents succumbed to the frantic buying spree surrounding these items. Somehow, we managed to secure what little remained. The journey was long, taking several hours, and my most vivid memory is savoring a Domino's pizza my mother had purchased on the way. Clutching my pillow, I drifted off to sleep swiftly, becoming ensnared in the realm of dreams.

02

WELCOME TO IAP

After enduring a tumultuous night that felt like a disaster, we finally arrived at our destination – and when I say finally, I mean it with every fiber of my being. A year ago, I visited this place, and I can proudly attest to the fact that the animal population has undeniably increased. Not due to cages, as we don't use them, but rather because of the cacophony of squawks echoing from the mighty old trees that serve as a haven for birds. These feathered creatures stay here solely for the food, while only the golden children remain, socializing with people. Some among them eat voraciously, akin to horses.

One of the puppies from my previous visit had matured into a dog, and it was none other than Kiki. He leapt joyfully, and I couldn't resist petting him. Meanwhile, my mom was in a state of panic after catching sight of Grandma sweeping away dust. Our home, a rustic, old house built by my great-grandpa, held a special place in my heart due to its boundless possibilities. The initial day of isolation was a sheer delight – no classes, no bothersome neighbours, no school; just pure relaxation.

Despite the modern interior, my parents wisely chose not to alter the exterior, a decision for which I was grateful. Reuniting with Grandma and Grandpa brought about warm hugs, and I proudly looked at a drawing I made of Kiki on my wall.

However, as the first few days unfolded, I began to realize that this situation was draining the life out of me. It meant no external or human contact, no sources of entertainment, and a strict prohibition from venturing outdoors. To add to the challenges, my mom had to work from home, engrossed in numerous commissioned artworks, while Dad assumed the role of chef until the lockdown lifted. Our kitchen, boasting a modern look, offered the potential for frequent culinary experiments with an oven and a microwave.

Amidst the monotony, my mind often wandered to the box containing great-grandpa's army equipment. Thoughts of guns and bullets filled my head, although they must be quite antiquated, given the aged aroma, appearance, and label that unmistakably screamed "OLD." The box, unopened since great-grandpa's demise 26 years ago, occupied a corner in our attic, housing other valuable antiques like a gramophone and an ancient vinyl CD music player.

We have a big TV connected to Netflix and all other OTT platforms which is the only thing that keeps me sane. I also have a lot of toys so I can be 0.00000001% entertained. If Grampa watches the news, I will just scribble something in my room. Yes, I have my room. When the painters came, I forced them to paint all walls except one in my room a pale, light green, which had faded a bit. Everything seems muted and pale, and even my energetic grandma seems sad. The world looked depressed.

Just when you might have thought we had overcome one dilemma, the reality was that we found ourselves in an even more significant predicament – the lack of any information regarding the mysterious virus.

So if you have noticed, Grampa is a child. Well, not physically: he is 75, but MENTALLY. He is a 7-year-old kid trapped in an old man's body. He too gives off tantrums. He too likes candy and sugar. He too gets hyperactive. He is everything that an old man can't be, but a kid can. He has this rusty room that is full of his awards and stuff. He also has a shelf full of Dad stuff (like newspapers, his old collection of cigar tins, photos of my Mum, aunt, and uncle, a lot of books, magazines, etc. and 5 or so bean body plushies he "borrowed" from my heaps of toys {which doesn't sound "Dad" to me})

You see, my grampa was a veterinarian doctor. From the day he retired (now it is 19 years hence, to be exact) this house has been a total zoo. The list goes on: dogs, cats, birds, etc. So he is still here, treating the animals, sometimes there, looking at the cats waiting for the stray dogs to pelt stones at them. He is not cruel, he just wants to make sure that everyone is safe because rabies is spreading in our village-ish town. My grampa treats the animals like his children and his children like....

No, not animals, how dare you! He treated his children like his children, dumbo!

Now the only thing which keeps me sane is my pets. My perfectionist gramma says that you only have time to study before marriage, or then you have to sit in the kitchen. She is a chip off the old school, which makes sense, since she married at the age of 17. But now child marriage is illegal, so I can sit peacefully till I join a nice university. Now I have a perfect 10/10 ground to defend my choices.

Working from home is a big issue. My mother has a lot of meetings and calls which slightly affects the quiet atmosphere of our house. We had to buy two headphones only to avoid sound pollution. I thought this was going to be the best vacation ever. But my fate was sealed and you can't change fate. So as I said, it's the repetition of the same day. My Dad is now coding and is talking serious stuff with serious people about serious topics for a seriously long time – later, he would get seriously grumpy, so no food experimenting. Seriously! At least Kiki can entertain me. I too love pets. I told you about the ones in school. So welcome to IAP: Indoor animal paradise. I am real about the IAP. You can also call it the IAS: Indoor Animal Sanctuary.

Oh wait for a second: did YOU know that my gramma is a crazy cat lady who cradles her kittens? Wait, I didn't tell you about that. Sorry, just don't tell Gramma about this. But anyway, my Dad made some paneer butter masala and some nice, soft, layered chapatis. That is

my favourite thing ever! The creamy, tangy gravy and the soft, mushy paneer combined with folded chapatis separated into soft layers is a chef's kiss combination; also my favourite. At our villa, we used to sit together for dinner at 9. But since Grampa SLEEPS at 9, we eat dinner at half past 7. So the schedule is completely changed. After dinner, I fed Kiki and the cats. Sometime later I played Twister by myself. I usually play these games by myself. This is one of the single-kid problems that I face.

03

FADING COLOURS

By the time the vacation starts, my village transforms with vibrant decorations, colorful balloons, and people donning festive attire. The air resonates with the sounds of bursting firecrackers, producing a whooshing effect, accompanied by traditional instruments like the chenda, ilathaalam, shanghu (basically a conch shell), and a kuzhal, resembling a pipe with a distinctive curve at the end reminiscent of a cut-out roller-coaster loop.

The focal point of the celebration involves majestic elephants, an integral part of uthsavams, Hindu mythological festivities centered around divine marriages known as mangalyam. Adorned with various items, four individuals ride atop each elephant. The foremost carries a vigraha of a specific deity, followed by another holding a venchaamaram, a white, fluffy brush. Then comes an alavattam, a circular ornament with patterns and peacock feathers, and finally, a muthukuda, a vibrant umbrella adorned with shiny decorations. In essence, the experience is truly remarkable.

The festivities also feature numerous stalls—around 50 of them—offering a diverse array of items, ranging from large to small, practical to trivial, sturdy to fragile, enduring creations to those with the lifespan of a fruit fly, and amazing inventions to questionable creations. Reflecting on my childhood when I used to feed the elephants, my perspective shifted after visiting an elephant enclosure. Observing their apparent joy in those confined spaces, I couldn't help but acknowledge the ethical concerns. Imagining a creature, much smaller in size, enslaving another for the entertainment of their own kind raises moral questions. Consequently, every time I witness an elephant in an uthsavam, a subtle sense of guilt washes over me.

The once bustling village now stands eerily silent in a deserted area. The allure of cities has led everyone to migrate, seeking a suburban paradise filled with affluence and abundant amenities. However, the reality is different—poverty persists everywhere, with a diverse mix of rich, middle-class, and poor individuals coexisting. Relocating doesn't automatically confer wealth or societal status; it's crucial to recognize limitations and ensure equitable resource distribution.

Cities are not the utopias of better lives as people make them out to be. A city is a very noisy and polluted place. And oh my, the vehicles. You can hear all the pent up anger of the people blaring from those poor vehicle-horns. The traffic jams are endless. The longest I remember had gone on for nearly 3 hours. And the rain water, when it falls, has nowhere to flow away; so it just stays there; dirty slosh. But city life does make everything a bit more accessible. Nobody uses this access for interaction though. In summary, in my opinion, city life sucks – a lot. But it is not utterly useless. Nothing is.

I am still trying to fit into this environment which feels so weird because I have lived here for like half my life. It feels so hard to fit in the silence because as I said, cities are very noisy. It was nearly midnight when I slept. The only sound I can hear is of the gentle breeze and the rustling leaves. All the other years, even drowsiness couldn't stop the firecrackers and music. But all that remains is tranquillity. In cities, a moment of peaceful silence is something people crave for. But now, here, it feels more sinister than peaceful.

Someone knocked on my door.

I panicked. Is that a burglar? If it is, why are they here? The only valuable things are my art supplies. Or is it a ghost? Or worse? A monster? Will it gobble me up? What would I do? My legs felt like spaghetti. I walked slowly, trembling in fear. Gathering all my courage, I opened the door. I slowly opened my eyes.

"Mum?" I asked, sighing in relief.

"Did I wake you up? Did you get any sleep?"

This is a trick question. If I said I didn't sleep, she will immediately send me to bed. But if I say I did sleep, again, she will send me to bed.

"I didn't get any sleep. This feels so weird."

"You are not alone, kiddo." She paused. "I am as tense as you too."

Don't worry, Mum. We are a family. If something

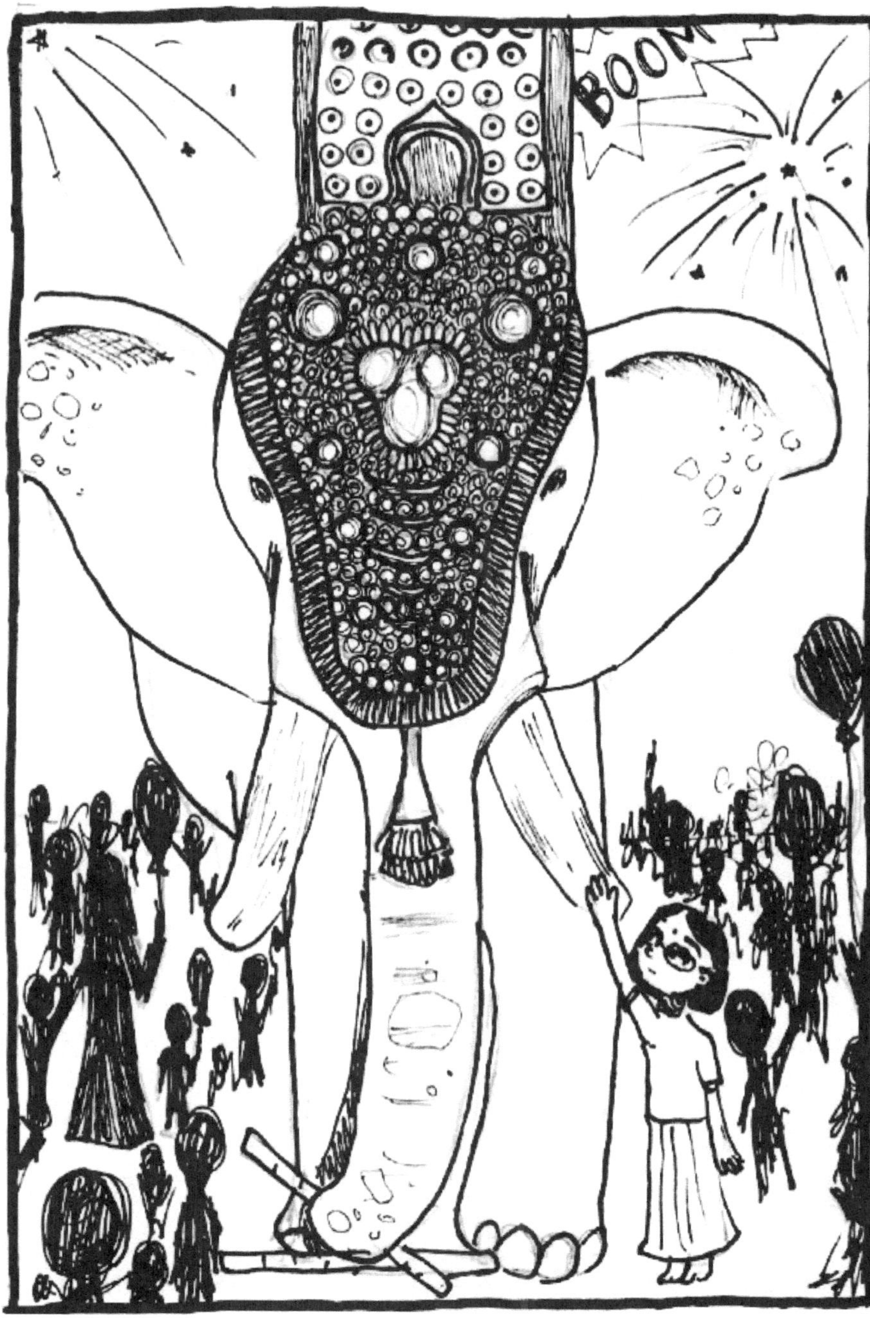
BOOM

happens, we will live through it together."

She hugged me and said "Everything will be okay." Though she tried to sound brave, I knew that she was crying inside.

I slammed onto my bed, which hurts a bit but I still like to do it. My Mum looked at me pathetically and said– "Once when your uncle did this, he missed and hit the floor. And he got 7 stitches the next day. Be careful."

"As I said, we are a family, we'll live through it together."

She did one of her fake smiles. It is unnoticeable for most people, but I know when she plasters a fake smile so I won't worry. Typical moms. I thought– "What I said might turn into a lie. We don't know what will happen unless a time traveller comes home and drops their huge history book, which will never happen."

Everyone seems tense. We have heard of the first death due to covid. We thought it will be like the flu, a harmless little epidemic but boy weren't we wrong. It has turned into a pandemic. My gut tells me that the following months will be a rocky road. Though it has been half past one, I woke up and drew a virus thing that is copy-pasted everywhere and I wrote the caption– the world will be like a new world.

I didn't mean it as they say in a happy singsong manner, but deadly serious. The thing with me is that whenever I try to sound or look serious, I sound or look stupid. One day, my teacher told me to speak about poverty, and when I did (a fatal mistake), I stuttered and mumbled and got everyone rolling on the floor. My friend Gowri asked what thing would I do which will have a great impact on the world (a homework question given by our English teacher), I said– "if I lived a few hundred years ago, I would've been working as a jester in a monarch's palace. So even if I did something earnestly, everyone would roll on the floor, laughing so much that it ached their bellies. And I am an embodiment of a jest. I try to look serious but always end up being stupid. So basically, I will make everyone laugh, even if it makes me look stupider than I am" I answered this seriously, and by the time I turned to see her reply, I saw her banging her head on our textbook to stop laughing.

It always happens to me. In our music class, I was "playing my violin" with my eyes closed in a sophisticated manner. It took me a long time to process that there was no music coming from my violin and when I peeped I saw two things–

1. My violin was held the wrong way the entire time
2. My entire music class, even my serious music teacher, bellowed with laughter.

I was so, so mad that I turned beet red in embarrassment. The worst part was that it was the try outs and my principal was also there. I knew this news was going to spread at the speed of light.

I tried to recall those memories. Rumours say that this won't end even after 5 years. I hope it does end before that. It sucks to be trapped in a joke for that long. I have heard that my parents had curfews in their childhood and THAT was enough to make them go crazy. So imagine being locked. Usually, vacations are so amazing and so cool but this ain't it. Though many things have made me go nuts, I may go really crazy once this ends. I hugged my pillow and curled up.

Again a knock on the door.

This time though, it was my Dad.

"Yes Dad? Don't worry, I didn't sleep." I said.

"That wasn't there when I came to call you for dinner."

I froze. Was it a ghost? A vampire? A monster? I turned reluctantly.

Luckily it was that virus ball thing. I sighed in relief. I hugged him and slammed onto my bed, as Dad shut the door.

04

VISHU

"So you are saying Vishu was not how it used to be, Gramma?"

"Yes."

"So how is it supposed to actually be?"

"Well first, there are stories behind the konna tree and the kanikkonna flowers. Do you know the stories?

"Of course not. I don't even know why Vishu is celebrated."

"Do you know the Ramayana?"

"No"

"Then there was this vanara named Sugreeva and he had a brother named Bali. Bali wanted to kill Sugreeva because his brother had locked him up in a cave while fighting a demon and he thought Sugreeva did that to be the king.

So Sugreeva asked help from Rama to kill Bali. And Rama shot his arrow at Bali from the branch of a tree. Later this tree came to be known as the "konna" tree because konna means killed in Malayalam."

"Well what about the flower?"

Well, the story of the birth of kanikkonna happens in the time when the caste system existed. The story is about a priest and his son who belonged to a lower caste. In their temple, they worshipped lord Krishna.

The son was always bored because there weren't any kids his age to play with him, but suddenly a young boy came from the back of the tree. The priest's son was surprised, because he had never seen a child, let alone a person in the temple than them. They played till dusk and the boy gave him a girdle made out of gold.

That girdle was strangely familiar but he still took it. When they reached home, he showed this to his father. Then a thampuran (a person of a superior caste) reached there and found out it was the girdle of lord Krishna himself. The thampuran, disgusted, threw the girdle onto a tree.

And suddenly, to everybody's surprise, the tree became laced with gold flowers. These flowers became known as kanikkonna."

"Now to the interesting part: How did you celebrate Vishu, Gramma?

"Well, this is like a farmer's celebration. By the time Vishu is celebrated, crops like paddy, bitter gourd, banana, cucumber, cashew, pumpkin, jackfruit, and mango will be ready to be harvested. We should use these to prepare the kani. We also put gold, silver and coins with the Bhagavat Gita or the Ramayana"

"So we are not supposed to like..buy things from the

supermarket?"

"Stupid rubbish you children are saying. Buy? There wasn't a supermarket in my time! Now they just put it up for decoration and put it on social media. There was no electricity or telephones when I was your age! If there wasn't any rice, we go and ask the people who have plenty if we can work for them. You can't just swipe a piece of plastic to buy rice, you should work for it! At that time, all houses, big or small, had rice. Either we will use rice from our field or the rice from the field we worked on. NO SHORTCUTS. A poor family had to go for reaping or threshing paddy from a rich man's house to get a handful of rice.

A rich family might not have some of these vegetables. So they think ahead and give some of their lands for lease. The person buying won't have to give money at first, but instead, they must give some of their harvests to the rich family. Then they will put all these together and prepare the kani.

The carpenters will give us a ladle and the blacksmiths will make knives and the coconut tree climbers will give us some green gram and jaggery and the grass cutters will give us grass for our cows if we give them a kainittam, which is just some money.

Then we light a lamp and quickly make some rice and curry and do a ritual known as "giving to Ganapati" in which we give a small portion of our food to a person whom we imagine as lord Ganapati. We will make an elevation out of cow dung. Remember the ladle? We will put some rice and crush some pappadams into it. We

will also sprinkle some water from a kindi. Then we will say while doing all this "Vishu kulichundoli" three times. When it ends, a person inside will eat the rice inside."

When we light the lamp before sunrise, we will show it even to our cattle. Then we will give the cows some sliced cucumbers and pumpkins from the kani.

After all this, we will light the firecrackers in all houses. There is also something called "kuppakkani" in which at sunset the day before Vishu and in the morning on Vishu, we set fire to all four corners of our land."

Woah, I thought; Vishu was certainly cooler back then.

I have seen 2 types of Vishu.

ENTER THE NORMAL 21st CENTURY VISHU-

Everything is store-bought. Not all things which Gramma has said are included. Just here for the social media validation.

NOW THERE IS.....COVISHU!

Till last year, we had something, but now we are broke, just a lamp and a piece from Mum's old yellow (which is more brown than yellow) sari. We didn't have any firecrackers so we had to rampage the attic to find-

Some moist fire crackers (which are as useless as skipping equipments without ropes)

Some snake tablets (that's what the box said, at least they weren't wet)

Well, I showed this to Mum and she said to burn the top. And when I did, it started fizzing and doing things. At the end, something like a deformed pool noodle came out of it. I looked at the packaging which showed a black snake with red glowing eyes when mine just looked like a burnt turd. That is the point of covishu. You are disappointed more than you can be disappointed. You experience boredom more than any other time (it is more boring than watching a person give a boring speech for an hour). Anyways, I got some pocket money as kainittam. It is a smash in my opinion. At least online shopping is available now. Otherwise I would've been dead!

05

THE TELEPHONE BOOK & MY COUSINS

You see, my grampa is this old man who always carries this old, musty, ivory-coloured telephone. He also has this big telephone book which was published like I dunno, maybe 20 years ago. He is sad all the time if one of his friends does not pick up when he uses the phone number that they owned 20-something years ago. Probably because all of them died.

My phone, which was my Mum's old mobile phone, is now in the hands of Dad. Well, at least my birthday is nearby and I will slowly coax my Mum into buying me a tablet or a mobile phone. Now I am the only phone-less member of the family (well the HUMANS in the family, excluding the massive amounts of pets). Or like last birthday, I will end up with a toy phone for a toddler. UPDATE- good news, my Mum bought a new phone and gave me her old phone. My cousins are jealous.

Speaking of which, let me introduce my cousins. I have three cousins; one is my brother Ayush who is the same age as me, then my sister Daya and her brother.

Don't let the name fool you though. Her name means "kindness" and she is absolutely the opposite. She thinks she rules me. But when any elders are around, she would be "sweet cute loving" and would be SAVAGE the moment they turn their back on us. She is like the ultimate soap opera villain. She would be like "Shiv you will get married to a rich man with lots of money and you both will get divorced and your husband will marry another woman" and so on, like she is the director of an Oscar-winning kind of dramatic soap opera.

She thinks she's a mature person with a mature brain and a mature look. You should see her near her neighbourhood kids, she puffs her chest and wears makeup that looks like a decaying goblin with bright pink lipstick and green and blue eyeshadow. When I sniggered after seeing her deplorable face, she said that I'm too jealous that she was cuter than me. She has a friend called Serah, who is the bossiest person I've ever met. She dyed a long strand of her hair to make her hair look as if Medusa was a pop star or something. She has the most atrocious accent like she's a world-renown celebrity. She always thinks she is smarter than William James Sidis when she's a feather-head who thinks that only outer beauty matters

I hope she gets expelled because she is feeding some really bad information to Daya. She always gives the excuse – I did that because Serah said that is right. I have never heard her say the same stuff about her

A fake photograph! It's my artistic talent!
NOTES
I'll scratch you in the face...
my face hurts from smiling
...again.
DAD'S BEST

parents. So I just mock her by imitating her by making an impression of her, swaying her hair, puckering her lips, speaking like she's a model, and all that stuff.

I would simply shove my hand into her face, nearly suffocating her, and be like "Shut up you little pest" One day I shoved her so hard that she fell, tumbling to the floor. I told her that "If you dare to speak a word about it, you will re-live this moment again"

Now you might think that I am a bad person. Let's talk about Daya later, okay? Nah, let's keep talking.

Her little brother is this little 3 feet-long energy ball called Vimal. He is kind of naughty, but more like my uncle, quiet as a mouse but with made-up stories big as a house. Speaking about my uncle, he can imitate Donald Duck. Also, Daya is greedy. She can't be more greedier. I give her all my intermediate art supplies and when she got one big hunk of marker with a duplicate each, she didn't even let me draw a flower. She says "Shiv, you always waste ink, it is worth 20000 rupees" I searched the entire internet to find that it's only worth a hundredth of her estimated value, 200 rupees, I don't want some crappy markers for 3-year-olds anymore, I've got better things to do with my life. But don't let her cute chubby face distract you; she uses all the markers to scribble on her hands and just washes it off minutes later.

Now all of you will be like "It's just your sister, your cousin, your younger cousin. So deal with it." Just go away, this is a whole different story, duh. NOW you might be thinking that I have an attitude: a BIG fat NO.

That's just who I am. What? You too have a younger (cousin) sister and you also suffer? Heh, well this cute round-faced overgrown American girl doll with an attitude must win the title "Time's most savage cousin since human existence began", like Albert Einstein, who won "Time's person of the Century ' ' in 1999.

Now, I adore her little brother. He only respects me, which makes everyone (including Daya, or, especially Daya) jealous. Daya's sister who's 13 however, loves me. Then Daya acts like she's "alone, sad, lonely, waiting for love". My mother then just walks in and spoils our moods excluding Daya's. Then she just thinks that my mother got me from the dumps and she is her long-lost daughter. Not gonna lie, Daya has got better neighbours to play with than me. Everyone here, especially kids my age, stares into my soul. Anyways, I can't ride a bicycle, don't come against me. Just asking: which kid rides a bike where there are traffic jams, accidents, and kidnappers + bonus, a nosy neighbour?

That's me. So she drags me around her neighbourhood, telling everyone that I can't ride a bike. She sometimes abandons me in the middle of the acres of paddy fields, full of mud. One day I nearly fell into a pit of gooey, stinky, black mud and ruined my trainers. Luckily, they are still here, clean and shiny. Now let me give rest to my restless mouth that complains.

GOOD NEWS! Grampa fixed my cousin's old bicycle and I'm now learning! I was just crying and angry because Daya made fun of me. I think he was sad and he somehow found the tools to help me. He always does anything to make me not sad. He didn't get enough time to spend with my Mum back at the time when he is swing double the time with me. I've heard my gramma say that my mother never knew the real difficulty of parenting because my grandparents spent more time in my babyhood than my actual parents!!

I, my grampa's grateful granddaughter, have made him a story – a memory game. The words will be the dots to connect to make the story.

The story took me a while to write, no lies whatsoever. I am pretty sure that Grampa will get annoyed by me. Thank you.

06

QUARANTINE

Quarantine, is a very fun-sounding word, isn't it? But not a very fun thing to experience. Ayush, my cousin from Ooty, has come back to our state- yay! And he is a physics whizz. So he and his family came home, and we told them to get out. Well, kind of. They used the stairs behind our house to reach the top floor. Then like those ring-throw games, we threw them the soap, sheets, sanitizer, and other things that don't start with the letter-' s'. As mentioned earlier, Ayush is exceptionally skilled in physics, demonstrating his proficiency by creating a functional model of a rocket. During his time in the isolation room (despite the ominous term, it is merely an additional room), he crafted a paper plane with a playful message that read, "Do you have any books on Newton's laws, nerd?" When I glanced up, I observed his mischievous grin on his somewhat unconventional face. Despite his playful antics, I decided to humor him and selected a book from my mother's reading collection that somewhat aligned with his specified topic.

He always asks for miscellaneous items from me, such as a pen or paper, as he enjoys crafting inventive contraptions. He often creates parachute-like devices to send items my way, and in return, I reciprocate by fashioning paper planes to deliver things to him. It's that simple. And because the "flexing-in-front-of-others-for-no-apparent-reason" gene is in our blood, he sent me these complex physics equations. Then knowing something (kind of) I asked him if he knows what any of these meant. Then he sent me an entire essay about that and I embarrassed myself- yay - for making me feel like an idiot in front of my cousins! Hip-hip-hooray! Hip-hip-hooray! Hip-hip-hooray!

Now, let's shift our attention from Ayush and take a look at the rest of my family. Currently, my grandpa bears a striking resemblance to those free-spirited hippies from the '60s. Thanks to the closure of barber shops during the quarantine, we've all been left to our own devices when it comes to haircuts. Speaking of which, my own hair has grown quite long, making it unbearable to leave it untamed, especially in the heat - I can't claim that it is hot outside anymore. Moving on to my mom, her eyebrows, which I'm used to seeing perfectly threaded, now appear as if they've been given an electric shock. It's somewhat amusing to see everyone going through their own struggles - I assure you, I'm not a psycho. Surprisingly, my grandma seems to be the only one who looks relatively normal. Meanwhile, my dad is embracing the salt-and-pepper look. As for Ayush, he opted for a DIY haircut from his mom, resulting in a hairstyle that resembles a bird's nest.

In other news, there used to be a colossal almond tree in our yard. However, when I was a toddler, an infestation of repulsive, speedy, furry worms that resembled vomit began falling from it like hailstones. Considering the unsanitary and unpleasant situation, we had no choice but to cut down the tree. After a lengthy process involving sawdust and eerie chainsaw music (which, if you're a heavy metal fan, you might appreciate as it's akin to a heavy tree being chopped up by metal), all that remained was a tree stump.

While painting our house, a very creative worker made a bigger tree stump out of cement around the old tree stump. He made it suspiciously like a cartoon character's home. Is it just me? I don't know. He filled it with the fertile soil of our garden and made it a plant podium.

Covid has kind of changed our lives, to be honest. We now look more like barbarians than cool-looking city people who have to act like they are absolutely fine (which is how we looked before the pandemic). But we're cool and chill. We just hide our pain inside like any other human (if you don't do that go search for other planets with life because your parents may have accidentally lost you here. [BONUS POINTS if your last name is alien])

I am now just sitting here on the floor. Don't judge me- they're clean.

COVID is super boring. I've already finished reading all the comics thrice. And there's like a heap in my grampa's room. When this virus first came to be, all the people who saw and heard the news, nobody knew this was a chronicle of a historical period.

Like I always wished for my teacher to say "OKAY DEAR STUDENTS, TIME FOR VACAATIOON!!!" but umm...I don't want a permanent vacation, and yay! That's what I got. Really, vacation and quarantine are two different subjects. Vacation time is when you can socialize and talk and travel and do cool stuff and vlog everything and make everyone jealous. Quarantine, my friend, is like being in a prison.

I don't want to think about this and go nuts, so I think I'll shut up..for now.

07

BIRD WATER SUPPLY

Hey. I'm back. Do you like being toasted by the sun? Then you will be happy because now the heat is slowly intensifying. It's like hell. So, I thought of the birds. Man, don't they suffer in the summer! They don't have ice cream in their refrigerators, smoothies, mojito, or even water. But yesterday, our golden-coloured kitten named Omelette (she's yellow and has a round belly, so when she lies down, she looks like an Omelette; hence the name) broke a pot. My gramma gave me an old curry pot. So, Grampa dug a hole in the soil and place the pot in there gently. We filled it with water and boom: IAP's first water supply. We hung a few pots in many other locations and filled them with water. While we were sweating, I asked Grampa:

"Remember what I told you yesterday?"

"What, I should stop eating candy?"

"No, about a story.some avian... creatures.other stuff.?"

"Ah yes!" he said, completely clueless.

"Okay then, elephant brain, what did I say?"

"Um..eh..AH! Grandma, Grandpa, and Tree.?."

"Well then, what was the sentence?"

"Once upon a time..a grampa and grandpa bird lived in a tree?"

"Awesome. Now, today's words are flood, rain and scared"

"And what about the sentence?"

"One day, a flood came with heavy rain. And they were scared."

"Okay."

"Can I ride my bike once more?" I asked, sporting puppy eyes.

"Sure do. I'll support the seat as you ride."

"Nah, I'm fine."

I started by putting my feet on the pedals. I looked straight and with a mighty puff of air...

WHAM!

I fell. My knee scraped and there was blood gushing

"HELP! AMBULANCE! POLICE! FIRE STATION!" My overprotective Mum screamed. So did a parrot, that was witnessing the accident from close quarters.

Mum used plasters and bandages and made my leg too heavy to lift.

"PERFECT!" she said, in a happy tone.

"Maybe that was too much.?." My father muttered, confused.

Now I am in my room, sitting and eating grapes like in those Mr. Bean movies' hospital scenes. No need for crutches though.

We hung the pots on our old banyan tree, amla tree, mango tree, etc. I also noticed Omelette, and Mongoose (it's a cat, don't be confused. She looks like she fell in ash, a silver colour. I have never seen that colour even though we have fostered a butt load of cats, same with Omelette) drinking water there as well.

They have a brother who is called "Son". You might think I'm dramatic but o, he lives up to his name. He knows these words: Son (his name), fish, nothing, out, no, and food. He knows how to open a door too. They are tabby cats and this apocalypse of tabbies started with a nameless cat, Son's great-gramma. She had many kids. Her mother died and she was the only one in the set of 3 to survive. She gave birth to triplets; one tom and two mollies. One of the mollies stayed and gave birth to butt-loads of kittens. At this time, someone said that she died. When there were many cats, two identical (well, sort of. One's fat and one is bony.) Twins stood out. The bony one gives birth, waits for 2 weeks, and abandons them like this is a makeshift orphanage with caretakers 10 times their size. The first two sets died, they were bony you see. And when she gave birth to these three, she was sick and died.

The other twin had two sets, a single kitten called Collar belt (more info about her later) and a set of triplets. Both she and the triplets immigrated to some place. She got her name 'cause the white line across her neck. The triplets don't remember their mother, but

MMUMM...
THAT LOOKS ALRIGHT!

they won't stop licking Son's tummy, thinking he is their mother. Son looks a lot like his mother though, not gonna lie.

Now you see the birds are HUNGRY and THIRSTY. See, I've done something nice during the vacation, ma'am: now I got an excuse when you say I am "irresponsible". I have nyctophobia, and I am proud enough to tell you. So, I have this little cat nightlight. Yes, you heard it right, I (a mighty soon-to-be 11-year-old / current 10-year-old) have a cat nightlight. My room is connected to my house, with a small hallway showing our beautiful orchids. So, I have my room full of feline stuff. I have painted a HUGE mural of a cat on a wall as well. My door hanger says "Pawdon me. I'm busy." And "I'm just kittening around". So, everyone must not furget to knock on the door. Got it: Yeah, furget, haha. Did I mess it up? Anyways, that was a jolly time talking about my love for cats. Oh, what? I have a whole lesson to write?! What a catastrophe! Just kidding, I just craved for another pun. Sorry if I've bothered you enough. Right now, I can smell food: Dad's cooking dinner. What is it you ask? It's my favourite combo. You don't know it? Well then re-read this entire book until here. That's a compulsory punishment if you forget that. Did you know that there is a condition where you can remember everything? I bet grampa will use it to condescend on me saying he does not have Memory loss.

According to my dad, our current situation is both a curse and a blessing. I'm not entirely sure what he means, but perhaps clarity will come when or if he decides to write a book about it. I'm no psychic, so I can't predict whether that will happen or not—just putting it out there! On a different note, my aunt recently gifted me a large set of polymer clay, and I'm absolutely thrilled about it. I'm contemplating what creative projects to undertake with it, and it seems I've settled on making cat decorations. Picture this: my room transformed into the ultimate feline apocalypse! MWAHAHA! But, to be clear, I'm not a deranged scientist attempting to control cats for world domination. Definitely not a psychic or a psycho. Got it? No need to suspect me; I'm just a seemingly normal kid who happens to be a bit... unconventional. Heh.

I have a library, connected to the hallway. Speaking of which, the garden looks like a painting when it's dawn. The sun rays peeking through the water droplets are just so very nice. Also, my grampa has been annoyed by me. Remember what I said when I wrote the story? I guess things are just falling apart. I already predicted that, but anyways, I try. And most of the time, uh, I fail.

08

AN UNFORGETTABLE LOSS

"Grandpa! I was searching for you!" I said, after seeing him watering the coconut trees.

"Geez, what?" he said, alarmed.

"Oh no, no nothing..".

"Oh yes, yes something is on your mind."

"Well, um..remember those words I told you?"

"Yeah, flood, rain and scared; and that sentence was like- a flood came with rain and they were scared and then then..".

"THERE'S NOTHING AFTER THAT!"

"Oh yeah."

"I think I need to train you to remember where things end."

"Okay this today's words are simple - baby bird, mama bird and papa bird, and the sentence goes like- then their grandchild, a baby bird and its parents, mama and papa bird came to their tree."

I walked away to watch something on the TV.

I am feeling anxious since Omelette has been missing for a day. We also noticed a broken pot which may tell us that there was a fight. We also noticed a pack of stray dogs roaming in our garden. I was anxious because she is the only golden kitten we have ever seen (not her fur (though she is), her loyalty and behaviour) in our years and years of feline fostering. Our maid was going to collect the peppercorns when she caught a FOUL SMELL. She went behind the rocks and saw the dead body of Omelette. This is not the first time strays killed our cats. All the cats that were killed by the strays had a missing leg, including Omelette. We dug a grave with a stone saying "Omelette: 1 August 2019– 11 April 2020"

Her siblings were also paranoid because we think they saw her being killed by the strays. Today morning, Mongoose went missing, but fortunately, we found her yawning and stretching in her bed, with her green glowing eyes.

Now there lies Omelette's bed, which is given to our cat,Collar belt. She used to sleep in it with a perfectly circular shape, which is impressive to me because I am a failure in gymnastics. Oops, I didn't mean to tell you I am a "failure" in gymnastics, but anyway, let's talk about Omelette. She always wanted to see our faces (or she tried to have head-to-head combat with us, who knows?) so she used to jump at our brick wall, making a quick, squelchy sound like blerch, the exact sound I make when I am in phase 1 of puking. She also raised her tail like a flag pole, twitching the end like a rattlesnake's tail. Also, did you know that a cat named Larry has the title Chief Mouser to protect the British president's residence at 10 Downing Street from mice? Mine doesn't even hurt a millipede. They would touch it once or twice and go away. Also, since Mongoose is a silver-ish colour, my Mum stepped on her when the Mongoose was sleeping on the pavement. Speaking of which, Mongoose has bright green eyes with contracted pupils. Her eyes only dilate when she is playing; that's when the cuteness starts to settle. Son is a gemwhen it comes to cuteness: both the kittens sleep in the perfect loaf position. They are smart too, I bet I can train them tobe world-famousskateboarding cats and I will become worldwide famous- dang, I forgot;

I.A.P TABBY CAT SECTION TERMS AND CONDITIONS:

Tabbies: Son (tom, 9 months), Omelette (molly, 9 months), Mongoose (molly, 9 months), Collar belt (molly, 11 months)

All the tabbies are grown under the protection of the I.A.P association of fosters. Rules*:

Cats must be fed 3 times a day, with a diet not containing grapes, raisins, chocolate, onions/garlic, bread dough (yeast), alcohol, xylitol, caffeine, liver, trimmings, and human medicine.

Water must be available under any circumstances. A minimum of 2 water services must be compulsory.

Beds must be cleaned and dusted once a week.

Cat poo must not be accumulated.

Do NOT feed rotten or stale food.

Cats must not be disturbed, forced, or abused under any circumstances.

*Rules apply to all cats. Terms and conditions apply.

See, see what I underlined. I wish I was a cat here, no homework, no activities, no onions; just eat, sleep, bathroom visit, repeat cycle. Sadly + the BIGGEST downside is that there is no chocolate, whatsoever. I better be a human then. Even my parents force me to do homework sometimes and I wish I was a cat.

Anyways, I started making feline sculptures. I don't mind the colour of the clay because I will paint it nevertheless. Speaking of which, I used this old paintbrush I sacrificed for using mod-podge for my wood painting as the lazy fur texture maker 3000 which I took from the dumpster. It turned out pretty good, pretty, pretty good. Now one is sleeping on my cot, and another is rubbing against my laptop. One is on top of my books, one is peeking from the window, and one is snuggling on my table-shelf thing, and so on.

My cats are sometimes so, SO camouflaged that we step on them. For example, Mongoose LOVES our pavement, cement stuff, and rocks. So we walk with a stick, like a blind man's white cane. Speaking of which, Mongoose looks like she has makeup on. Black lines on the end of her eyelid look like they're eyeliner and her black lips look like black lipstick. Do NOT judge me, I HATE make-up. I am allergic and I have either crusty skin like a roasted potato or pimples like an orange: Better safe than sorry, duh.

Meanwhile, Daya does NOT stop picking on me even when I say to her that she is getting on my nerves so much that I just wanna bite her head off (that's a phrase. I am not a psychotic cousin. Believe me.). She will be like "You have ugly skin. To fix that, you must buy some foundation cream and apply it with a sponge, no, not the sponge you wash your nasty dishes with, silly, but the one shaped like an egg" or "You have dry and chapped lips. You must buy some lip water or you won't look nice, Serah said that to me when I sent her a photo of yours and she said- is this a baboon?" or "Every girl must love make-up. What you are doing is a sin. Serah says that makeup makes you look like a model, not an ugly, drooling ape" with her fake model accent. Once I told her (before the shoving phase) "I will hit you in the head with a rock...hard" a bit too loudly, perhaps; oops. She started whining and wailing and blubbering and cursing me (really.). I got scolded by both my parents and her parents. And after an ear full of what a sister should be and what a sister should not be advice,

09

THE MUSHROOM DEN

"Grandpa! Wake up!"

"What? What happened?" He asked when I stirred him from his slumber.

"Do you remember the words I told you I don't know, few weeks prior? Those three, extremely easy words?"

"Ah, that nuisance again? Let me sleep a bit, kiddo." He mumbled as he hid inside the blankets.

"Please...aren't you a good grandpa?"

"Fine then..um..baby..mother and father something.."

"And what is that something?"

"Cows? Buffalos? Cats? Dogs? Oh Birds!"

"Alright what is the sentence?"

"Would you not ask that if I give you that huge packet of chocolates?"

"But there aren't any, grampa.."

"Okay, um.their grandkid baby bird.uhh.,.its parents, the mother and father bird....came to the tree?"

"Good. Now you may go back to sleep."

He happily continued sleeping at the speed of light.

Woohoo—now it's the monsoon season: which means slugs (yuck) worms (double yuck) creepy crawly stuff (triple yuck) cold (no thanks) mushrooms (eh.) a completely new and boring online academic year (NOOOOOO!) and my birthday (Yay!)

But my birthday is way, way far from the school opening. Yes, I am underage for a normal 6th grader and younger than the kids. That's why I am using my brain to think about brains and help my grampa restore his memory. Speaking of the brain (wow me, what a bad transition), here are two (one creepy and one for arguing with your parents) facts that YOU didn't know (even if you did, please say you didn't for my namesake, can you please?)

It was a banger when humans found out that the human brain controlled the body by using electricity, especially for an Italian doctor named Giovanni Aldini who decided to experiment with this with some headless criminals. Their limbs twitched, mistaking the electricity for the electricity the brain sends. A young author named Mary Shelley wrote a creepy book about a dead body scrap monster named Frankenstein inspired by this incident. She wrote it when she was 19 if you wanted to know.

You may have heard that you only use 10% of your brain. Did you think it was right? If so, you're WRONG. You use your entire brain but at different times. Also, your brain capacity is unlimited. USE YOUR

BRAIN!!

Now, I hate the monsoon season, to be frank. Because of mud, wet, lightning, thunderstorms, floods, tsunamis, and [insert a bajillion other things you hate about monsoons], on the bright side {sorry to all the other kids reading this. My Mum forced me to not be negative when I can be positive, so sorry.} Monsoon makes you feel cold (a bit queasy to me, personally) and does not let you be completely scorched and fried in the sun (very bad for lactose intolerant people who has rickets). Monsoon rain provides excess water to plants (which may destroy them, or worse start a flood) also, rain is a major source of water (with free viruses and bacteria in it, I suppose) to all living beings.

But yesterday we had a thunderstorm SO BAD that mushrooms sprung out of every inch in our plantain, yam, taro, coconut trees, fruits, and veggies farm. Yes, I know it's a very hard name to spell, let alone memorize. But you will get the answer when you see it. I am not the kind that teachers use as role models like the ones who lived with wet and mud and rain. I hate it.

My Dad bought me a pair of crocs (the shoes which have holes and make your feet look like duck flippers.) I am a pale, thin, and underweight kid so my legs are thin as a stick. Now Daya calls me DUCK FEET, ugh. Now she has another thing to harass me with.Ducks don't have a blob as a foot, instead, they have webbed feet. She's an idiot.

Now let's get back to the topic (which is mushroom hunting btw.)[And btw means by the way btw]). We got nearly 3 buckets full of edible fungi grown on decomposed stuff; which may sound icky and gross and terrifying when you hear it. But it may only take you a second (if 1, you aren't stupid or 2, you don't know what saprophytes are) to realize it's just a harmless mushroom (or it won't be if you are taking a scrumdiddlyumptious [a word invented by Roald Dahl, which means delicious and lovely] bite out of a poisonous and inedible mushroom, jeez. Good luck living after eating that deadly poisonous death cap[Amanita phalloides, it's a deadly poisonous basidiomycete fungus]). You will have vomiting, nausea, diarrhoea, and even scarily, DEATH.Man, I didn't know a literal mushroom could kill you. So I hope we didn't harvest our DEATH. I don't know why I am so intrigued by DEATH. Whelp, that's the third time I said dea.l.mean "the word".

Now you might be asking (no, you didn't? umm.).

Wait..grampa is right there..I got my prey...

"GRAMPAA!!! Let me tell you today's words!!!"

"Not this again, Shivani.?. he said.

"Come on! It's so easy!! They were scared of the flood but went through it as a family. And the words are scared, flood and family!"

"Fine.?.

10

PARACETAMOL

UPDATE: there's this new terror, aka online classes. The problem was ehh... 6 whole hours of online classes. I thought there weren't any. I'll never be THIS disappointed ever again. However, I've realized that this century is definitely better than its predecessors. So, old is not always gold, guys. Watch out.

We are a LOT luckier than the people who lived in the MIDDLE AGES. And I mean a LOT. First of all, instead of COVID they had the plague or tuberculosis, but 10x more deadly because hygiene wasn't a thing. There was no TV, Smartphones, or Wi-Fi! Like what?! And as the icing on the cake, there were psycho kings and queens who chopped people's heads off, for "ENTERTAINMENT PURPOSES" and jousting. Speaking of it, did you know that King Henri II of France got poked in the eye by a MASSIVE SPIKE while jousting? And he died because it damaged the prefrontal cortex? What a Nightmare! Ugh, now thinking of it, my brain feels lousy.

Speaking of which, the usage 'feeling lousy' came to

use because they thought it was due to lice exploring your scalp. But the reason why they were thriving though, is because there was no HOMEWORK (it was invented in 1095; smack dab in the middle of the Middle Ages)

"Hey Grampa! Can you come here?"

"The words are scared, flood and family and the sentence is 'They were scared of the flood but went through it as a family' "

"Whoa! Grampa, you have improved..now let me tell you this today's words are suuuuuupper easy! They are ups, downs and normal. And the sentence is- They had ups and downs but believed it was normal"

"These are a bit easy.?.

I have bad news. Guess what I got up to? Your girl went out to fetch mushrooms without an umbrella. You can guess what happened next. I know, my friend, have the TWO MOST COMMON COVID SYMPTOMS: FEVER and COLD. So, my Mum went out (cough cough) to buy me (cough) Calpol, or Paracetamol, if you still live in the 19th century. My Mum dilly-dallied a bit, and then remembered that I was her daughter.

So, (cough) thanks mu-(cough) I-I mean thanks, Mum! My Mum said I should apply steam to my throat and chest. It just makes me look sweaty. Now that my temperature is skyrocketing to the max, I can sit lazily, having Calpol and reading comics. But here is the ugly list of thumbs-downs-

THE UGLY LIST OF THUMBS-DOWNS BOO!!

No Netflix (who even made that rule? Anyways, boo scale: 10/10)

No engaging with pets (understandably. They do leave fur and fluff balls which may make you go achoo! Achoo! Boo scale: 5/10)

No school or homework (at least one nice thing boo scale: 0/10)

If this used to be back at home, Mum would just buy some bread; make me some garlic bread using creamy butter and garlic, baked it in the oven, and paired with a citrus drink. On some special days, Dad will make me a very creamy soup, sometimes tomato soup with croutons or manchow with fried noodles. Speaking of fried noodles, there used to be a restaurant at a junction nearby. It was named ' coco bistro' and it was where I celebrated my most recent birthday in. They had many posh dishes such as Chinese mushroom gravy, Bluebarb (Blueberry Rhubarb) crumble, etc. But their most stunning piece was honey-glazed tender chicken served with fried noodles. Before any more gibberish, let's time-travel a bit. Let's go a bit back..where are you? Nah, not last Easter, a bit more...where are you now: Dinosaurs? Nope, you're a bit too far. Just a little bit more..Perfect! Where are you now? 1878? C'mon!

Here we are, 1878. A year before lazy ol' Tom Edison made a light bulb and two whole years after Grubby Hands Alexander Bell made a telephone, a bloke named Harmon Northrop Morse was in his early 30s making tablets – specifically, Paracetamol. My Dad was teaching and screaming at people to teach the right way to build a website when HE was in his early 30s.

He was a normal bloke, spending massive amounts of time researching and doing stuff. More importantly, he has a cooler and more interesting name than Isaac Newton. He was also the cause of a very terrible joke, it was not made by him, nor was it offensive. Uncles in 1878 started telling a joke. Imagine this: I walk up to you (or sit beside you near the fire, if I was an uncle in 1878) and ask you, "Why aren't there any medicines in the jungle?" what will you expect: hopefully not the answer. It is because the parrots eat ' em all; probably not the best. Then I'll laugh hysterically in "Dad".

So now we are saved. Yay! Speaking of which, do you ever think of the entire universe being reset? And there's this whole new big bang? And nobody remembers us or our creations? If that sounds eerie, imagine if it had already happened and people used to live in the future a few billion years ago and just..vanished.

STAY tuned for episode 2 of Shivani's uncanny thoughts causing mental trauma!

Also now, I just have to hear the lousy speech of some student from my class, I was too lazy to look at her name because I can make an excuse that I will strain my eyes when I look at the screen. But that will be a backlash while I borrow the TV to watch Netflix.

11

MY BIRTHDAY

Finally, it's the day I've always wished for, my birthday!!!! But it's not like my usual birthdays which I celebrate twice (one in school and the other with my family). Till last year, I gave sweets to others in the class and saw our principal, and heard a lecture about life and spending it wisely, and making wonders on the earth. Then she takes the large book with photos of hundreds of students who are in the navy or army or who are actors or chefs or scientists or whatever. Then there is the disconsolate, insipid, and bitter "Happy Birthday" song. A classic. And now there's a parody for it.

Even though it's my birthday, I will still train grampa to be undefeatable. Here we go again (sigh)...

"Grampa.Grampa! Do you remember the words?"

"I think they were...um.uh...ups...downs.and normal? And the sentence was "They had ups and downs but believed it was normal"?"

"Good job Grampa! And here are the words for today– hugged, saying and okay. The sentence is um.Sometimes they hugged each other, saying that everything will be okay."

Then when we go "home" we must dress and prepare expeditiously. Then we go to a restaurant and cut a cake and all the distant relatives say their usual dialogues– "Oh you've grown up so much! You start to look like your father so much, doesn't she?" as they look at their miserable children or cousins or siblings or spouses, waiting for a yes.

But it's like they are trying to plaster a fake smile on their face and try to hide the fact that I have grown less than an inch in a year. Then Ayush always puts the icing on my face just before we get out of a restaurant and cleaning it takes a jolly fifteen minutes because that scoundrel always puts more than a little icing on my hair as well. Then Mum and Dad force everyone to eat a massive amount of food.

Now things are different. I sit on my chair, hearing the gloomy song again. Why can't COVID remove that? Luckily I didn't start the day with my Mum screaming her head off.

Then we still have a cake. A home-baked one that is. It was chocolate. It was a bit burnt. But it was chocolate. And chocolate is good. So I drew a cacao bean with a crown and it was sitting on a throne made of cake. Then there were the other cake flavours, kneeling and begging for mercy or praising him. No, I am not weird. I am CRAZY. Then we had Mum's tripod with our mobile phone set up, having a live meeting with our family members. Then we took photos of me with my parents and grandparents. What I am trying to say is that it feels quirky to be going out and having fun and immediately being confined into a house in the span of a few hours is a "10/10 would not recommend this scenario" if your dumb mind somehow thought it was fun.

I opened my gifts. Do you remember when you were a kid (please seek help if you were not a kid once in your life) there used to be these huge art kits full of art supplies, which looked like Davinci's painting supplies but you took your words back when they met paper and turned out to be the crappiest thing in the existence of human beings. Yeah..that is what I got, despite being 12 years old. PATHETIC but I did get some nice art supplies though. Even Daya was not able to come because of a curfew or something, I think. But I am not at all sad because she didn't come. She usually is the one who spoils my party by covering my face in icing and making me look like the abominable snowman from the Himalayas.

There was this polymer clay kit which is very useful for making things out of. I also got a sketchbook and some watercolours. Still, we made my favourite food, guess what it is, I am not going to tell you. I reached a personal record- reading the same book one hundred times and still being sane.

Daya had made me a birthday card and it read- "Happy birthday to my second dearest cousin!" which makes no absolute sense because I am her only cousin. She also drew a picture of me which does not look like me, at all. But the more I look at it, the more it looks like me. Now I am questioning myself: am I that ugly? Fortunately, Ayush was not here to mess up my face and hair this time. It was such a setback to wash your face

PPY BIR

but still get bitten by ants because some icing got stuck behind your ear.

The weird thing is that I miss those days of freedom and happiness even though I have been teased and made fun of a little too much by my cousins. I was kind of happy on the first day of lockdown, which sounds very weird to me because now I wish to go outside to meet other human beings. Though I am a person who enjoys being alone, this is too much, even for me.

I "borrowed" Mum's birdwatching set and took the binoculars to look outside. I can see faint, wispy figures which look like ghosts. I am pretty sure ghosts are not real, but if they do exist, I just saw ghosts. Then I can see a few cars, which might be a person buying groceries for their family.

This is not the happy, colourful town we lived in. Everything is gloomy, grey and looks...weird. It almost feels like we live in a whole other place.

I closed my eyes and thought this was all a dream.

A dream where I did not live in that crappy villa

A dream where covid did not exist

A dream where everything used to be happy and colourful

I woke up from the trance when grampa called me, asking how the microwave works. Thanks for letting my imagination to not work, grampa.

I only remember now to tell Grampa the sentence, but meh, it is too late, because it's midnight.

12

HOW MY GRAMMA CAUGHT A TURTLE

"Grampa! Grampa! Grampa! Over HERE!! DO YOU REMEMBER THE WORDS???" I screamed, when I saw him doing something ten metres away.

"Stop, Shivani! It is 4 in the morning! Let others have some sleep. Oh and the words were umm..hugged, saying and okay. Sometimes they hugged each other, saying that everything will be okay"

"AMAZING!!! Also today's sentence is the easiest on the planet. No, the easiest in the Milky Way...No, the easiest in the entire universe! Days, weeks and months passed; that's the sentence. The words are days, weeks and months. Now let me go and sleep."

"You woke up just to ask me this silly little thing?"

"Silly? How is this even silly? I am doing this for you, grampa!'

"Anyways, go and sleep if you don't want your head bitten off by your mother"

"Oh yeah.?!

"Also don't tell her what I have just said...you know the reason why."

I nodded as I walked towards my bedroom.

Do you remember Daya? Well to show her and my parents that she's a loving sister, she gave me fish. We already have guppies and she took them from my farm and gave them back to me. Nobody feels anything sus, but me. But like always, I can't say no. I just had to plaster a fake smile on my face ratherthan say "Oh, ew! Go away you menace!" Even though I'm stuck with fish, my grampa used to have a pet chameleon and my gramma used to have a turtle and a water dragon (one of these pets may not be true).

I just put them in the medium tank because guppies see their smaller friends as quick, delicious, and healthy snacks. Imagine if that happened to humans too...

Like, you are afraid of your mother because she'll eat you.You are afraid of your father..because he'll eat you.You are afraid of your friends and family..because they'll eat you.

STAY tuned for episode 3 of Shivani's uncanny thoughts causing mental trauma!

I have these Santa Claus guppies. They are just laid back dudes with green bodies and white and red tails. Speaking of pets, my elder brother has a Persian cat and Daya has a Maine Coon! I like them because again, they are just smarty-pants laidback dudes who are as big as Daya's brother.

My gramma was born in 1960: her mother, who already gave birth to two boys, and her father, a middle-aged man who had another wife previously. She was the apple of the eye of her father. She was a handful. She tells stories of having glass stuck into her foot causing an infection and her catching a turtle and other useless activities.

One day when the fields flooded (which nobody was paranoid about) my gramma went with a glass jar to catch the exotic fishes in the fields. According to her, it was a hobby back then. People used to dip sarees to catch bigger fish. So she caught a fish and noticed a turtle! She immediately took it, showed it to her father, and plonked it into the well. Yes, into the well. Then she said it was never to be seen again. Like imagine, only well water and a turtle are dead. Imagine all the dirty stuff you eat with it! OH, EW! GROSS!!!

She lived her entire teenage without any ELECTRICITY. I can't imagine such a life where there's no YouTube or Instagram or Snapchat. It's SO BORIIIIIIIIINGGGGGGG AND LIFE DRAINIIIIIIIIIIIIINGGGGGG...

Also....my pappus plant has been soooooooooo big! I know right. I got it sneakily during a boring science explanation at school. Wanna hear the story?

My science teacher Greeshma was teaching us how different plants disperse seeds. At the same moment, a pappus came out of nowhere. The entire class went crazy to catch that. But she just shushed andwhile we were stunned she snatched it in one go. I was right in front of her because I have vision problems, thus the glasses. A boy sat next to me, and I just ignored him. So the seed slipped from her hand while she was showing it. She didn't see it. So I took it and hid it in my geometry box. That boy was like TEACHER SHE..but I just stomped him on his foot. Now that was over 5 months ago. A lot has happened in between, right?

P.S. if your answer was "NO" then please re-read this book. Also just go to a neurologist to check if you have Memory loss.

13
BUTTERFLY HATCHERY

I have never, ever seen a kitchen garden in real life, until now. You see, my gramma spends HOURS in the kitchen garden just to come back with barely anything. So today, I set out with her to unfold the mystery. She was just throwing away all the worms...until I noticed some caterpillars. So we had a tiny talk which went like this:

"Hey gramma, why are you doing this?"

"Oh, look at these pests! They just feast on my curry leaves and citrus trees."

"Well that's a butterfly caterpillar", I said, re-checking with the help of the internet.

"Anyways, I got to throw these away, or we have to skip curry."

I want both, so, a light bulb lit in my head. I went to the house to find an empty jar.

"Here", I said. "Put them here, I'll raise them."

"Oh no, you won't! You never do the right thing twice!"

I sighed. "I will this time, Gramma. Now, please, give me those caterpillars."

By this time, grampa entered the scene.

"GRAMPA!!!!!!!!!! The WORDS!"

"Days, weeks and months passed; that's the sentence. The words are days, weeks and months....I think?"

"Correct! The sentence for today is Things seemed to get worse by time and the words are things, worse and time. Also, can you give me some curry leaf things? I want them for my caterpillars!"

"Okay..How many?"

"Five or six would last for some days."

So, butterflies. There are many stories about them. I like the story "And then there were butterflies", which I fished out from the internet this evening. Please note that this is a North American mythological story. I will summarize the story for you here:

The first human twins were born. Their mother, Spirit Woman relied on the animals to look after them (lazy Mum). After a while, they figured out something was wrong. Even though the babies have turned into toddlers, they refused to play and run with all the baby animals. They confronted Nanabush (Nanabozho), the cultural hero and spirit god who helped to create the world to find a solution. As the Great Spirit called his name, Nanabush followed his instructions and gathered pebbles of all colours. He threw them into the air and they turned into tiny winged creatures. Mesmerized by this, the twins stood up on their own, running to catch these fluttering butterflies. As the animals saw this, a smile appeared on all their faces.

This may not be scientifically accurate, but still. Who hates stories? Yes, you at the back with a terrible haircut don't like stories? Sorry, nobody wants to hear your opinion. I am not a fan of those overly exaggerated fairy tales. Fairy tales are for disgusting, ruthless kids who are oblivious to all the catastrophes happening around them. I, like most kids, am obliged by my parents to read books.

Anyways, back to butterflies.

You may know the life cycle of a butterfly, probably. If not, I pleasantly invite you to Daya's classroom which is now learning about metamorphosis. Anyways, what you may have never heard of is the camouflage of freshly hatched caterpillars. They look like a sick bird took a great crap on them. When they peel their skin off (really) they will turn leafy green. Also, they are a lot more easily annoyed than they were (like you). So they will show their red horns and release a funny, puky, and disgusting door. I am starting to have second thoughts, to be honest.

Oh, at last! The butterflies had made their cocoon/pupa/chrysalis so here is a gruesome fact about not-so-lucky number 3; butterfly edition

GRUESOME FACTS THAT YOU REGRETTED LEARNING

PART-I

You see, when the caterpillar makes its cocoon, it doesn't just sprout wings and come back and be like "Hi hello nice to meet ' ya!"

They turn them into this pus-like liquid. It's like a very gooey juice-BLEUGH, DISGUSTING, GROSS, NASTY, FILTHY.

You're welcome for being creeped out so much that cold shivers are passing through your spine. More fun fact, they can still remember everything before turning into goo. Jeez, that is terrifying.

Now you'll be like: Why in the freaking existence of the world are you so immature talking about poo and puke and

gloop. All I have to say is:

Y E S!!! I thank you for understanding my real behaviour and cooperating with me. Now I sincerely ask you to just LEAVE.

Thank you.

Okay, So far so good. To be honest, it's so hard to be sane in this irksome pandemic. At least some people are enjoying this.

Now my grampa and I are playing Snakes and Ladders (the only game here that I haven't touched).Oh here comes a tiny talk between us

"Ah, Tomorrow is Atham (a Malayalam star) in the month of Chingam. We must make a Poothara (a platform made of cow dung and soil. Btw, Poo means flower, you can digest it in both meanings, either a platform made out of poo/a platform made out of flowers. Choose your option according to how revolting you are.)."

"Why? We can just do it on the floor right?"

"Well, we believe that we must make the Poothara and the Thrikkakarappan (a stone) must be placed, sandwiched between two tulsi leaves, and will be surrounded by umbrellas made of hibiscus flowers."

"Man, we didn't do anything like this from the city."

"HA! I won!" he said. I noticed that he moved a space extra, but I kept my mouth shut and smiled.

Man, our culture is so colourful and fun. Now tomorrow for the first time in my life, I am going to make a Pookkalam (flower carpet) from the flowers of our garden! I am so flabbergasted! Good night!

14

ONLINE ONAM

Now I am here, in my groggy mood for fun, I just rode my bike to fetch all the flowers. My grampa was following me behind because of um..the previous incident. All the flowers were sleeping and were dehydrated. So we stopped till the sun rose (yes, I did wake up that early).

My grampa started saying:

"Do you know the story behind onam?"

"Do you remember the words?"

"The sentence for today is Things seemed to get worse by time and the words are things, worse and time. I don't forget it, see?"

"Oh, and today's sentence is: But one day, a tiny boat appeared in front of the tree, and the words are day, boat and tree."

"Okay, now let me ask you: Do you know the story behind onam?"

I shrugged.

"You see..there used to be this asura (monster) king

who ruled Kerala. Unlike other asuras, he had a very kind heart. In his time, all humans were treated equally. Everyone lived harmoniously together. There were no threats to happiness.. There weren't any pandemics or child deaths. The storage sheds were full and all the crops were treated the same. The evil was extinct and only the good remained on the earth."

"Damn. It just sounds like the world before Pandora opened the box."

"Stop interrupting me with all your itty bitty YouTube nonsense that those freaky people in your phones feed your brains." He said.

"Okay and um..Isn't it 6? I think we should get some ideas."

My grampa replied very rudely by spitting a ball of saliva and toothpaste into the backyard. I took the greatest tool of them all..My iPad.I opened my weapon of choice-

DIGITAL ART.

I first showed the outline, then the colours and the flowers to use.

"Eh. Too pink.

Too Yellow

Too warm

Too boring

That feels too right.

That's a common one

Just tweak the colours.

Those colours are too clashy.

Maybe make them more of..same

That just looks like one colour"

When I looked up, my grampa was staring at me, with toothpaste on his faint moustache.

(AWKWARD SILENCE)

"Huh," I said. "Looks like I started the problem."

"It's 9. Get ready for your ONLINE CLASSES" Said mom, entering the scene.

"NOOOOOOOOOOOOOO!!!!!!!!!!!!!" "I don't want to!!!!!!!!"

"DO YOU WANT ME TO RAISE MY VOICE?"

I kept my mouth shut. I don't want to see her beast-face.

"But I want to make a Pookkalam," I said

"Tomorrow's Saturday." She said, sighing.

"FINE," I said, reluctantly.

See, this is why I hate this school! My cousins are now enjoying their vacation.

UPDATE! All my classes were cancelled because the teachers just made us celebrate. I was too tired and left halfway through. What can they do? Put me back? Send me home? I can't! I am too..tired.

I overslept. When I woke up it felt like it was 7 in the morning. But there was something weird about this morning ... (My brain had forgotten the catastrophe that

happened before). I was so fed up with the bitterness in my mouth that I decided to eat breakfast.

I took my brush and noticed my cycle outside the porch, near the flowers.

"Huh. That's weird." I put it back in place.

"Shivaaaaaaaniiiiiii…". I trembled. It was DAYA'S VOICE.

From my mouth the Toothpaste-saliva mix dripped to my chin…

I turned

"What?"

"BWAHAHAHAHA!!!!!YOU ARE BRUSHING YOUR TEETH! YOU LOOK AS HORRIBLE AS THAT CIRCUS MONKEY WITH RABIES I SAW YESTERDAY"

"So what?"

"IT IS EVENING!! 3 PM. This is not morning! YOU OVERSLEPT, YOU BOZO!"

Great, I thought. One more thing for her to harass me.

It's fascinating how there are words we need but aren't recognized in official dictionaries. These are known as sniglets, a term introduced by Richard Hall in the ' 80s. Singlets find their way into the Urban Slang in vogue. The perfect sniglet for my current situation is "napnesia," cleverly combining "nap" and "amnesia."

Acting as if nothing happened, I proceeded to unpack the lunch. I believe Daya arrived with my uncle, or some other elder. Meanwhile, my parents are at the grocery store, busy purchasing essentials. Grandpa and grandma, true to their routine, are napping. We had chapatis, because –

1. My grampa has a high chance of getting diabetes

2. My gramma wants to look like a model, rather than a plump, old lady.

It's too cold and stale.I.can use this as a Frisbee, or a weapon to injure Daya with..ugh. Why? My family eats lunch at 1:30.

I took the bread loaf and garlic butter to make some garlic bread. Daya stole them when I made mine. So I ran behind her until she gave me the unwanted crust. I threw the crust with some dirt in her pink dress and her face because I was too cross. Just kidding, I ate it, Kids, don't waste food.

I washed my hands and made another batch. I just added some of my secret ingredients to make it much more delicious. I also just roasted a few vegetables (it's the best combination ever!). By the time I went back, Daya was playing on my mobile phone. Let's just pray for the phone that will be dead by the time she gives it to me. I just sat at the dining table and read Harry Potter because I am the nerd in my class. That is also why my cousin harasses me a lot.

Now the regulations are being loosened bit by bit because the number of covid patients is decreasing. Mom says sooner or later we will go to school. Which will be much more entertaining than staring at these blue screens all day long.

"Here, take this phone, shiv."

"Okay, now what?"

"Gimme the TV remote."

"Only for 10 minutes, okay?"

"To watch some lame channel for nerds, maybe?"

I didn't act like I cared, I wanted to look tough in front of her. My eyes nearly ruptured and bled when I saw this message–

Dear students of Oakleaf™,

Happy holidays!

Since it is the holidays, our school has assigned different classes different assignments. The 6 compulsory writing assignments are attached to this message. There are also 8 mandatory activities that include observation and research. 10 optional activities are also attached. These ten will substitute your marks if you will get low figures on class tests. So if you got below 75%, it is mandatory to attend all 24 assignments.

ENJOY YOUR HOLIDAYS WITH CREATIVITY, WRITING, OBSERVATION, AND RESEARCH!!!

Regards,

Ms. Boring

Class teacher

Yeah, enjoy. What were the sour–faced principal Mrinalini and pouty–faced teacher Ms. Persephone Marceline Clementine Magnolia Priscilla Whitlock (aka Ms. Phoney) thinking?

I shut that thing off in horror and went and sat with Daya.

"Hey, Shiv..would you mind if I tell you something?"

"Go on.."

"I am sorry.for calling you stupid, gas lighting you, spreading rumors that you are disabled because you don't know how to ride a bike, telling everyone that you are an intruder because you look different than everyone in my house, abandoning you in the vast fields.."

".and I am sorry for calling you a pig-faced jerk..you know what Daya, you made me "me". I draw better now because you said your brother can draw better, I cook better now because you said that sand and gasoline tasted better than my pudding, and I sing better now because you said that I sounded like a cat puking, I am tidier now because you said my room looks like it just went through a tsunami. I even learned how to ride a bike because you said that I am not smart if I don't know how to ride a bike. You pushed me to my limits, Daya. You made me believe that the sky's the limit."

My uncle barged through the front door. He thanked me for babysitting Daya. I giggled when Daya punched him in the guts for saying that. For the first time, she hugged me and said goodbye.

"The world changes when you change", I thought.

POP QUIZ! What was the full name of Ms. Phoney? No looking. Yes, you with the permanent monkey face – Correct! You win 1000000000000000000000000 rupees (that's one septillion right there)

Don't spend all that buying stuff! It was a joke! You didn't spend it, right?

I hope so.

15

POPPY THE DEAD

You should've remembered that the regulations are less strict. Because of that, my other cousin, Ayush, decided to visit his family in another district. He has a red Siamese fighter fish called poppy, with a black belly. So when we look from the bottom, it looks like a flower. He was tense to leave the fish alone with his grampa because he either neglected or smothered something a bit too much.

I understand his feelings because my gramma fills everybody's tummies a bit too much when they visit us. So when my parents say that I'm greedy and I should give them more cookies, I just say- better safe than sorry, I don't want to be the contributor to diarrhea..or diabetes..or both...

He sent me all these photos of him visiting the beach, shopping, gobbling down food, and all those stuff to make me jealous. Just to mock him, I sent photos of me swinging, playing video games, painting, cooking, and all those things with the same ugly smile of his. That telltale told my Mum and voila that here I am, grounded. At least he got what he asked for.

But he forgot about poppy. After his entire trip, he returned, and to his bad luck, he saw her dead and flipped upside down. His previous Siamese fighter fish, daisy also died while in the hands of his grampa. After he got out of his depression, he started investigating. You see, his grampa is a bit too compassionate to creatures, also he misreads everything because he prefers squinting his eyes to figure things out embracing the fuzziness rather than wearing glasses. So instead of feeding it 2 grains 2 times a day, he fed it 22 grains a day, so instead of 28 grains a week, he fed it 154 grains a week.

You see if you take a musty old history book and flip to the rulers' section, you'll see many, many names like Francis I, Louis XI, Elizabeth I, and much other gibberish. So I, the annoying cousin I was, named it Poppy the Dead, hehe...

Ayush was so, so mad that when I said that in front of him when he visited my house, he chased me with a slipper for about 30 minutes. After our parents settled the rabid dogs in us, Ayush gave me a card that said–

"You are dead, but long to be forgotten

POPPY'S FUNERAL:

Time: idk

Date 22/11/20

Venue: The damp backyard that is forbidden"

"What in the world is this trash? I asked

"A worm is smarter than you.Can't you just read? It's poppy's funeral!"

"What should I do?"

"Come, duh."

"I think you're too naive to mimic my attitude, but anyways, I'll come."

"Also, why have you not SEEN MY STORY??? You are so disrespecting that you didn't even budge to send a message saying three letters?"

"B Y E, U O K, or W H Y?"

"No stupid, R I P"

Now I am in the damp backyard, and it's a mess. Ayush's pet parakeet screeches "The best day ever" in ' SpongeBob Square pants'. I nearly had a panic attack thinking that Ayush will have a double funeral because he threatened his parakeet, grass (because it's green) with a carving knife.Daya was very emotional and bought a wreath and Ayush made a gravestone out of wood. I just know that the termites will have a grand feast.

Let's just get out of these baby games because I am the eldest. I just said to Ayush that this funeral is so disgusting that I could barf because Vimal, Daya's brother can make a funeral better than this. Ayush again told my Mum, but she just ignored it because she was too tired to digest everything.

"GRAMPA!!!"

POPPY
BORN : 15 MAY 2019
DEATH : ? UNKNOWN
(GRANDPA DOESN'T SAY)
Here lies poppy,
whose fins were so floppy
Now lying underground,
He sleeps so sound
Let him take my love,
Soaring with wings above.
Rest In
Peace.

"Here I come, and the sentence is: But one day, a tiny boat appeared in front of the tree, and the words are day, boat and tree."

"WOW, GRAMPA!! You are outstanding! Also the sentence for today is: They were sceptical but they decided to take the risk and the words are sceptical, decided and risk. Got it?"

As you may have noticed, it's NOVEMBER!! Nothing interesting happened between these months so I decided not to bore you, wow me! The time I spend with Daya is more fun because Daya and Ido not despise each other. Vimal too is young enough to play with us, so he always creates a mess. So instead of painting and stuff (which can go wrong if Vimal is there), we can play other games like pretend, statue, or I spy. Since I am not a person who is interested in running and jumping and stuff, and Daya isn't, sometimes we fight, but nobody is injured like what happened a long time ago.

Speaking of fish, you know I have guppies, right? If you don't just reread the entire book until you reach here. That is a compulsory punishment. So I bought this big thing (I don't know the name) shaped like a flower and made it like a pond, with sand, stones, and other things. It is very big and I put all the adults in it. The guppies are just straight-up hyperactive. I am thinking that a guppy's blood consists mostly of Red Bull.

Also, they like to play hide and seek. They will hide between the crevices of plants and stay still. Then another fish will head-butt the hiding guppy.

Life is awesome because we only have one, but things

don't always go to plan, because we are not living in a fairy tale. There will be ups and downs, pros and cons, dark times, and bright times. But the only rule is to find happiness in everything, because if we don't, then what's the use of life?

Covid came, and everything was locked, so what could go wrong, right?

16

BAD HAIR-DAY

I was so, so wrong. My hair was getting so long it was JUST above my waist, so my mother told me to get a haircut. Daya just got a haircut to match one of her friends. No offense, but she looks ugly with curtain bangs and a haircut that makes her head look like an egg. So, my mom took me to a nearby salon instead of our normal salon. The ambiance was okay, I guess. But OH MY GOD MY HAIR IS MESSED UP NOW!!!!! I just look like that eggdog meme! UGH! At least yesterday was the last day of school! Imagine me walking around looking like an egg! Everyone would laugh at me! But the worst thing is that an 80-year-old snail can beat my hair in a race because it is slower than that snail! I think I dozed off or something. I woke up when my hairdresser put the blow dryer in full heat and started melting my scalp off. My Mum screamed in horror as three-fourths of my hair was lying on the floor. Anyways, myMum got so angry that she didn't even look at the person who hands your bill.

You see, the problem is that my hair is wavy and it jumps up a step for god knows why. So even though my hair was shoulder-level, I look like an egg because of my hair. Ugh, I hate myself so much. At least it is easier to look after my hair. Instead of a two feet long jungle full of tangled vines, which take hours to brush, and again turn into a mess, you can just brush it in one go! Easy! But now my gramma is very sad because she says this makes me look sick (in a bad way). Anyways, now Daya and I look like two puppets

Everybody wants to hear what happened and then I have to narrate this tragedy, and I have to hear all their sympathetic responses and act like I feel better after hearing their words and all those nonsense. As it can grow back, imagine it was your leg or something, you're no lizard to grow it back! Once one of Mum's friends went to pluck her eyebrows and it ended so badly. At least that wasn't me there! Also, Daya didn't make fun of me, but just said we look like twins. At least there's peace between us after Daya and Igot along. Now, she makes me laugh!

"Grampa! Grampa!"

"They were sceptical but they decided to take the risk and the words are sceptical, decided and risk. See, I do not have memory loss!"

' Okay, Grampa! Chill! The sentence is "They rowed for what it felt like a hundred years and the words are rowed, hundred and years." – I think Grandpa is cheating or something because I start to feel that he's better than me!

This is the most trendliest cut here!
You like your new stylish haircut?
boing boing
You look So Cute with this style!
.....

17

CAMPFIRE, HOT CHOCOLATE, AND A CHRISTMAS EVE

Today is Christmas Eve, one of the best days in the entire year. Uncle, Aunt, Daya, and Vimal never forget to surprise us. Uncle already came home this morning. He boasted that we will have a campfire and a warm mug of hot chocolate at midnight. He is a fibber so I didn't mind but oh boy when I said this to Daya and added a sarcastic note that Uncle always does what he says. She took it literally and threw a tantrum. My uncle went to our shed and got some firewood. We lit it to make a fire. My Dad, an old scout, managed to place them like a cone. The hot chocolate was so good though. Dad just took all the ingredients, did some sorcery, and served it to us in about 8 minutes. Since my uncle put the campfire beside my bedroom, I just sat there and watched. Daya went all hysterical and started screaming and dancing, especially after draining an entire mug of hot chocolate in under 1 minute.

I have a teepee tent inside my room and Vimal was inside that. I was looking outside my window, sipping hot chocolate. My Dad was half dead and both the Mums were not so crazy about celebrations so they three sat on my couch. After a few minutes, I heard my Dad snoring. It was both funny and sad at the same time. The Mums were chattering, not even minding my Dad.

That's when I heard Daya scream "AAAAAAAAAAAAH!!!!!!!" Everyone (even my Dad who woke from his sleep) dashed to see if she was burning or if a snake bit her. She said- "the time is 00:05, I forgot to wish you merry Christmas, ma!" she said. Dad groaned because he was so tired. Gosh, sometimes the girl just does absurd stuff.

Anyways, the spirit died down a bit. I was making a Christmas card at midnight because why not, Daya was binging Netflix on her Mum's phone. I slept for about 14 hours today because I sleep like a hibernating bear when it's vacation. I just finished the card and I just put it on my humongous desk. I just stick this card and make another card when it's the New Year. The wall in front of me looks like the one police officers use to collect photos of serial killers, victims and other gory stuff.

I don't know why, but I had a strong urge to eat pizza. I kept my mouth shut because I knew Mum would say I only eat junk food. Vimal was like he breathes, eats, and drinks Red Bull. Speaking of drinks, I hate soda, I just don't know how I like the feeling of burping. It just makes me feel queasy and like my stomach just twisted and turned, which can happen with organs. Ugh, now my stomach hurts more. At last, uncle decided to go back home because it was 1 hour into the birth of Jesus.

SNORE
.....

And of course, both Mums didn't forget to wake up Dad in that noisy process like always. Poor Dad, he woke up and just walked away slowly to the bed, moaning because he didn't get enough sleep.

I however was very energetic. I was pretty scared to go out because I have severe nyctophobia, and even walking in a dark room makes me feel queasy, even though Mum says it's babyish to have fears. I might've taken it deeply if she didn't have any fears, which is not the truth, she fears standing at a tall height, you should've heard her scream when we went trekking two years before, she screamed and I thought that my ears nearly bled.

You see, I am glad I am a single kid because you must see the dark circles that my uncle and aunt have under their eyes. Imagine a kid that is so hyperactive that they practically scream in their sleep, my uncle has two of them. Poor uncle suffers a lot. Daya was so, so, so hyperactive when she was a babyish toddler, but Vimal is 10 times more energetic. He hates sitting and I can just see future-him struggling in school because he is so eager to get up from that nasty chair.

Anyways, I am now lying in my bed, thinking if a person is looking out of the window, or if there's a monster waiting for me to open the door, or if there is one under my bed. Scared out of my life, I shut my eyes very tightly. Even when I hear the leaves rustling, I just panic, thinking this is my fate. On a cold, windy night like this, I lie on my bed, I try to sleep, all curled up, hiding in my blanket because I am scared. I am always scared, I am a coward, and I always was. I stood out from the mighty, proud, selfish, and jealous students in my class, rather than talking about movies or series or shopping or makeup, I always stayed alone in a corner, with my face buried in a book. Coward, even my friends say that, so brittle and pale, always afraid of something. Even my parents are now scared. Scared of the new virus, scared that something will happen to us, scared that we will starve to death, scared that we will lose our loved ones, scared that this won't end, scared that we won't make it until the end, life is tough, a never-ending roller coaster, with loops, peaks, and all other nonsense.

I was awake the entire night, staring at the sky, a bit more relieved, looking at the different stars in the sky. I was looking at a pale white star, with four slightly bigger stars around like they were trying to protect the pale one. The five stars were twinkling weakly. There I was in the center, I thought, so weak and brittle that I know my family can't save me. I also saw that as time passed by, all stars got weaker, and weaker and weaker. I got lost in my thoughts and stared at the sky for a while longer, and then I hid under the blankets once more. I thought of my family and my loved ones. Even though I like being alone most of the time, I can't live without them, they're my family, and I can't lose them. I looked at the sky once more. When all the stars were flickering weakly, the same five stars were the only ones who were bright in the sky. A small smile spread across my face when at last, I hid under the blankets, feeling happier than ever.

As I woke up, more refreshed and earlier than usual, a smile spread across my face. I walked through the hallway, more enthusiastic than ever in my life. I took my mug full of coffee and sat down on the couch. Even my parents knew something was different. I wished them good morning with a warm smile. Instead of fighting with grampa for the TV remote, I just gave it to him. This was the first time I felt how it is like to make someone happy.

18

VACCINATIONS AND MY DEATHLY FEAR OF NEEDLES

I am deathly afraid of needles. The fear of needles are known as *trypanophobia*. Either you are scared of needles or you don't care. If you say that you like sharp little things and being jabbed by them, I won't believe you. People who like needles are not humans.

Anyways, let's just talk about needles (thank me for putting my blood and sweat and tears into speaking about a subject that I hate as much as broccoli). Back in the 17th to 18th century, smallpox spread like wildfire, causing lots of people to die from it.

Enter Edward Jenner: an English physician born in 1849. He discovered that women affected with cowpox never got the much deadlier smallpox. He then collected the disgusting pus by popping the gruesome boils (ugh) and then injected that to the 8-year-old son of Edward's gardener, James Phipps. When he injected the smallpox virus sometime later, the boy survived.

The word "vaccine" originated from the Latin word

"Vacca" which means cow. Now this was in England. My grandparents have also gone through this epidemic. My grandpa was born in 1945. So he went through a horrible childhood stricken with poverty, diseases and other things. When he narrates the things that he went through, I think being locked in this house is better.

In his childhood, when somebody got smallpox, there was no blister pus, no vaccines, no treatment, nothing. They fell into a feverish coma, and then, they were just..... buried alive. Even if it is your loved one, a newborn, or a really, really, old man or woman, if they were in a coma they just...buried them alive. But it wasn't that bad for the conscious people. They will be isolated in a house (remember quarantine?) and a person who had already got smallpox and was cured of it will help them with food and all because they are now IMMUNE to it (I really suspect it is superman wearing someone's skin).

Now I have a question-

Why are white mice used for vaccination experiments? They are adorable!

Well the answer is that even though we look and act completely different from mice, we have a very similar immune system with mice. I still don't know why they are adorable. Ayush is always having a panic attack when he sees a mouse because in his posh school, there aren't any mice, nor in his villa. We had a lot of thoughts, but they are rats, they are ugly. Speaking of ugliness, there is one animal that is both ugly and immune to cancer- the naked mole rat. It looks

ORAL HYGIENE,
OVERALL HYGIENE!
Stay calm!
CLEAN
TEETH
BRACES
ARE
ACES!

as disgusting as it sounds.

Oh and one old funny thing about mice-

When we came from town to this house one time, we bought some momos for our grandparents to try. My grampa opened it and said- "are you trying to kill us by making us eat little white mice?!" It took a bit of time to make him understand it's not a mouse. He is like a child when it comes to compromising things. I bribed him with some old candy which was nearly 2 years old and has expired, because it has been nearly two whole years since this ruckus has started and grandpa got diabetes a few years prior to covid. It must have been given by one of our neighbours when something special happened or something, I don't know.

Anyways, it is getting closer and closer to our final exams and my biggest fear is that because of this vaccine, we have to write the exams from school. And I hate it now because I have to smush myself into that crammed room of mine in our villa. So I am praying to god even though I am not that religious that school doesn't reopen. But on the bright side, I am so, so, so excited to meet my friends!! It is such a bummer that we had been locked in. they have changed a lot! Some have gained weight when some didn't, yada, yada ,yada.

These past few months have been a great lesson to me. And let me share what I have learnt so far. First of all (this is a warning) let me tell you that I am no big person like those motivational speakers who know philosophy and those kinds of boring old things. This is also the reason why I am an idiot when it comes to speeches. The only speech I have ever said about was the most amazing thing in my childhood: candy. It was a class assignment or something and I got a D grade because my language was rubbish and my speech promoted children to eat candy. This would've been great for the dentist because they would get some money...I think. But my teacher called my parents and said not to entertain my behaviour.

Anyway, I got distracted. Let's continue the topic. What I was going to say was that life can take you down strange roads and the biggest example of this is the covid pandemic. If you were to tell me that we were going to be locked up with no human contact and entertainment, plus there would be online classes when I was eating chips with my friends on the last day before the finals when I was in 5th grade, I would've believed that you were mentally insane.

Even my worst nightmares, such as living with Daya for a week wouldn't have frightened me as much as the news of online classes. If you really think about it, life is both weird and amazing at the same time.

Here comes my grampa, unsuspecting of me.

"Grampa!!! The words!"

"Oh um...Ha! You thought I forgot it, didn't you? Well, the sentence is they rowed for what it felt like a hundred years and the words are rowed, hundred and years."

"Aha! Well, the sentence is: But from all the darkness and cold, they saw light. The words are darkness, cold and light."

19
COPYCATS

Oh, I forgot to say that my cat collar belt had two kids. A black one with orange eyes and one that looks just like my cat Omelet. Then, mongoose gave birth two weeks later, and um, they too look the same. So I got a pun, copycats. Hehe. So I named them the following–

1. Coal
2. Omelette II
3. Charcoal
4. Scrambled eggs.

I am so, smart and sane to name them absurd names right? Wait, what did you say? What, only the most insane person will name a cat scrambled eggs? No way, because I am sane, at least, that's what I think the truth is. Being absurd may sound funny to you, but the truth is said in 3 simple words– Oh, hell no. Being called a psychopath is not fun. I am absurd in many ways, but not even half as absurd as my cousins. Ayush always carries a knife for fun, and Daya dyes her hair pink using oil pastels

What just happened...? Are they...
COPYCATS!
PHOTO COPIER
Hullo!
.....
INDEX
45 GSM
A4
PAPERS
A4 PAPERS

to mimic Serah, a person I'm sure you've forgotten. If you haven't, yay, and if you have, reread this entire book out loud and consult a neurologist. Even I am tired of being absurd, which may sound absurd, which again feels absurd and this goes till the world ends. I am now inside my room, trying to write a story about my pathetic life in 2020 full of sanitizer, social distancing masks, and other gibberish. Both my class teacher and mother say to me to write something good, rich, fruitful, positive, and beautiful (if you know what that means.)

I could've written a Shakespeare play last year IF I had a single brain cell in 2020, but now it's 2021 and I'm sitting here, looking out the window to see if a tornado is coming, looking at the sky to see if it's falling apart, waiting for tragedies so I can finish this huge, damn diary my Mum bought me to improve my language. Like I can't even survive on my own and she says I need to improve my language? First, teach me how to sweep the floor or to clothe the folds, I mean to fold the clothes, or how to make food,Mum and then I'll improve my language, stoopid parent stuff, right? Children these days are getting spoiled because parents are buying them anything they want, doing all their work for them, helping them with their studies...You don't agree with what I say? Come on, don't lie.

Now I sit here in silence, waiting for something to happen. Imagine if I tamed a tiger to maul Ayush, or grass the annoying parrot rapped "rap god" and got a world record, or if Serah got a role in a movie as a spoiled brat, or if Ayush gets a life sentence, or if I find a new species, or if school reopens.

"Grampa!!"

"Well the sentence is: But from all the darkness and cold, they saw light. The words are darkness, cold and light."

"Great job! And the final sentence is: They checked if it was safe and then finally, flew towards the sun. The words are safe, flew and sun."

20

A MIME'S STORY

"Grampa! We did it! The final sentence!"

"Well umm..I forgot it...".

"What?"

"You fell for it! Okay the sentence is: They checked if it was safe and then finally, flew towards the sun"

"And the word?"

"Safe, flew and sun!"

"Is there any cheating here?"

"Oh no, Shivani! Why would I do something like it?"

Let's cut to the chase and stop beating around the bush.

Usually, we think that butterflies just turn to their winged forms by the magic of Tinker bell or something. Well, some people in fantasy stories have butterfly wings bursting from their backs. How is that even possible? It's as logical as Serah being the smartest person in the world. You can't just have layers of chitin outside your body (sorry to all arthropods, insects, and fungi reading this. My sincere apologies.)

You know mimes. Those black and white guys with stripes all over them. No, not prisoners, I mean those dudes who act like mutes and try to escape an invisible box. Poor guys. Even if something bad happens, like they choke or have a heart attack, we just think it's their amazing skill of acting. That was very dark. So what happens if you mush up the butterfly and mime together?

YOU GET the common mime.

Its male looks like a mime, thanks google. I got one of its caterpillars and now I'm trying to make it hatch. It's very tedious.

First, their eggs are 1mm in diameter, then they'll hatch and eat their eggs and then, they grow and grow until they'll be nearly 5-6 cm in this length. Now they'll shrink and change color and do weird stuff. Then, their cocoon will disguise them as a stick. So basically, it is boring. Imagine having a spider looking like a clown, that kind of disappointment. Like, butterflies should be extravagantly colorful so we'll say that those in children's books aren't photo-shopped. Also, spiders should be black, white, and gray, not like they just tasted the rainbow.

There are many butterflies, more than 17500 species. Butterflies are found in every continent except Antarctica, which makes sense because it's way too cold. There are butterflies in all sizes and colors, from every color a kindergartener knows, from teeny tiny wings to humongous wings, there is every butterfly you can think of (except one with neon yellow and neon purple with neon orange and neon green spots [that's probably because it doesn't exist]).

So, that means that you can think of absurd butterflies which can't even exist in a parallel universe. Speaking of butterflies, do you know that common mimes rip parts of their heads while they turn into a cocoon? Mother Nature was like – off with the outer shell of their heads!" I also decided to name my soon-to-be butterfly "pain"

21

EVERYTHING MUST COME TO AN END

Not everything can go as you planned. World isn't a paradise. Nothing can be controlled completely by humans, like how the weather forecast can be wrong or how your mother burned your pancakes by the slightest, and more. But the thing is if you are always bitter and pouty about every single thing that happens, then you may feel like your life is a punishment. But if you learn to enjoy your life, like how you can sit inside your house the entire day because nobody knew it was going to rain, or still cover that burnt taste with a ton of maple syrup, you may enjoy them. The point of life is to step outside of your comfort zone.

For example, if you lived in a house made out of cotton wool and wore a tracksuit made out of marshmallows and a beanie made out of feathers, and one day you dress like a normal person and go to a normal place, you may get a bruise or a cut or something. If you cry and complain about it, you will just continue to live in a hole.

But if you just move with it, sooner or later, you'll get used to it.

This virus made me learn a lot of things. If we decided to go somewhere else, we would've never learned any of these. If you ever want to change your past, you won't live the same way you just did. Like if you went and corrected the forecast, you won't be able to get a day off of school, or if you took the pancake just before it got burned, you won't get that extra dose of maple syrup.

The government told us that we could go back to school, which meant everything I bonded deeply during this time must be left behind. My pets, my grandparents, my bicycle, my "pain", my joy. We tried our best to find alternatives and to live with my grandparents but it was out of our control. We had to go back to that crummy villa. We had to pack everything. My little ecosystem was destroyed. I sobbed as I had to pack everything into my bag.

Even though the doge stickers on my diary made me laugh every time, this was the first exception. I looked at my shabby little bicycle. I hesitantly packed everything and kept it in the back of our car. It seemed like everyone was having a bad time. A few minutes ago, I saw my grampa fiddling with it but now he's here, without the bicycle. I went in to check "pain". "I hope you'll turn into a beautiful mime, little friend," I said, with a touch of pain and sadness in my voice.We hugged each other(Not the cocoon you weirdo, the humans. It would've burst and fill my hand in goo). We said our goodbyes in such pain that it felt like somebody was stabbing us in our hearts.

We started our 6-hour-long journey. This was the time when I realized that we felt the same like a butterfly in a cocoon. No, not turning into juice, like we wish to pop out of that cocoon. So badly. I hugged my pillow and looked outside the window. Everything has changed. Our small village is now on the path of becoming a concrete jungle. The extending roads made me hurt. I knew this won't be the look of the village when we come back. All of this will disappear. It will look like every other city. I looked outside. I didn't know when the time passed. We stopped and ate gramma's food. I won't eat such good food for the next few months.

We drove and drove. My crying stopped by then. I looked out. The usual landmark, the infamous "Raja" tea shop was there. Then came our school. A few meters later, there was our villa. We went in the gate. We opened to take the car to take everything. That's when I saw my bicycle, neatly covered in newspaper, with a letter – "I hope you will take this to school every day. With love, grampa". I hugged the letter. It had the smell of the dusty old paper he uses. The tears of both sadness and happiness rolled down my cheeks.

Wait..another letter? I looked at it. It said–

"Once upon a time, a grampa and grandpa bird lived in a tree. One day, a flood came with heavy rain. And they were scared. Then their grandchild, a baby bird and its parents, mama and papa bird came to their tree. They were scared of the flood but went through it as a family. They had ups and downs but believed it was normal. Sometimes they hugged each other, saying that

everything will be okay. Days, weeks and months passed. Things seemed to get worse by time. But one day, a tiny boat appeared in front of the tree. They were sceptical but they decided to take the risk. They rowed for what it felt like a hundred years. But from all the darkness and cold, they saw light. They checked if it was safe and then finally, flew towards the sun.

P.S. I used to write the story here and read it just before you came. I hope you won't be angry with me because I wrote each sentence trying to remember what you said."

Oh, Grampa. Why would I be cross with you? Deep down, we are just a granddaughter and a grampa.

As I walked into my bedroom, I took some duct tape and stuck both these letters on the wall. Not only do these letters show our relationship, but it also recalls the covid memories.

"THE WORLD CHANGES WHEN YOU CHANGE"